THE GREAT AMERICAN CAROUSEL

THE GREAT AMERICAN

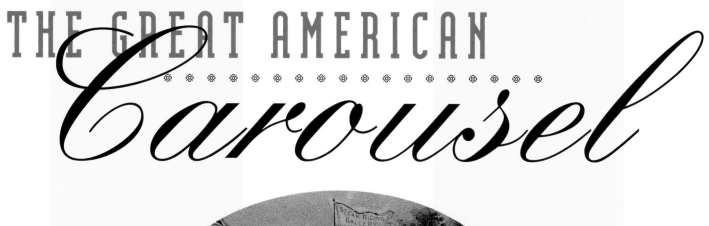

Carousel

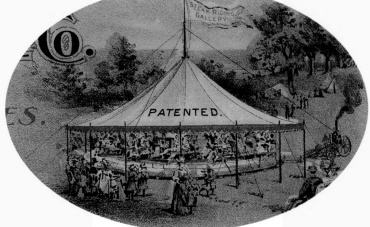

A CENTURY OF MASTER CRAFTSMANSHIP

BY TOBIN FRALEY

Foreword by Nina Fraley

CHRONICLE BOOKS

SAN FRANCISCO

Printed in Hong Kong.

Book and cover design by Lisa Levin Design.

Library of Congress Cataloging-in-Publication
Data:

Fraley, Tobin.
    The great American carousel: a century of
master craftsmanship/Tobin Fraley; Foreword
by Nina Fraley.

        p. cm.

    Includes bibliographical references and
    index.

    ISBN   0-8118-0610-3
    ISBN   0-8118-0634-0 (pbk.)

1. Wood-carving—United States—History.
2. Merry-go-round art—United States—
History. 3. Animals in art—History.
4. Woodcarvers—United States—History.
I. Title.
TT199.7.F73   1994
731' .832—dc20   94-1370
                              CIP

Distributed in Canada by Raincoast Books
112 East Third Avenue
Vancouver, B.C. V5T 1C8

10 9 8 7 6 5 4 3 2 1

Chronicle Books
275 Fifth Street
San Francisco, CA 94103

Table of Contents

Acknowledgments....8

Foreword by Nina Fraley....11

Preface 15

CHAPTER 1   Carousel: The Concept....18

CHAPTER 2   Coming to America....28

CHAPTER 3   The Golden Age Arrives....38

CHAPTER 4   A Day at the Factory....58

CHAPTER 5   The Master Carvers....68

CHAPTER 6   Daniel Carl Müller: The Craftsman as Artist....76

CHAPTER 7   Loss and Rediscovery....84

CHAPTER 8   Carousel Doctors....94

CHAPTER 9   Old Methods, New Animals....104

CHAPTER 10   More Than a Merry-Go-Round....112

Afterword....122

Bibliography....125

Carousel Census by State....126

Museums and Displays....128

Index....130

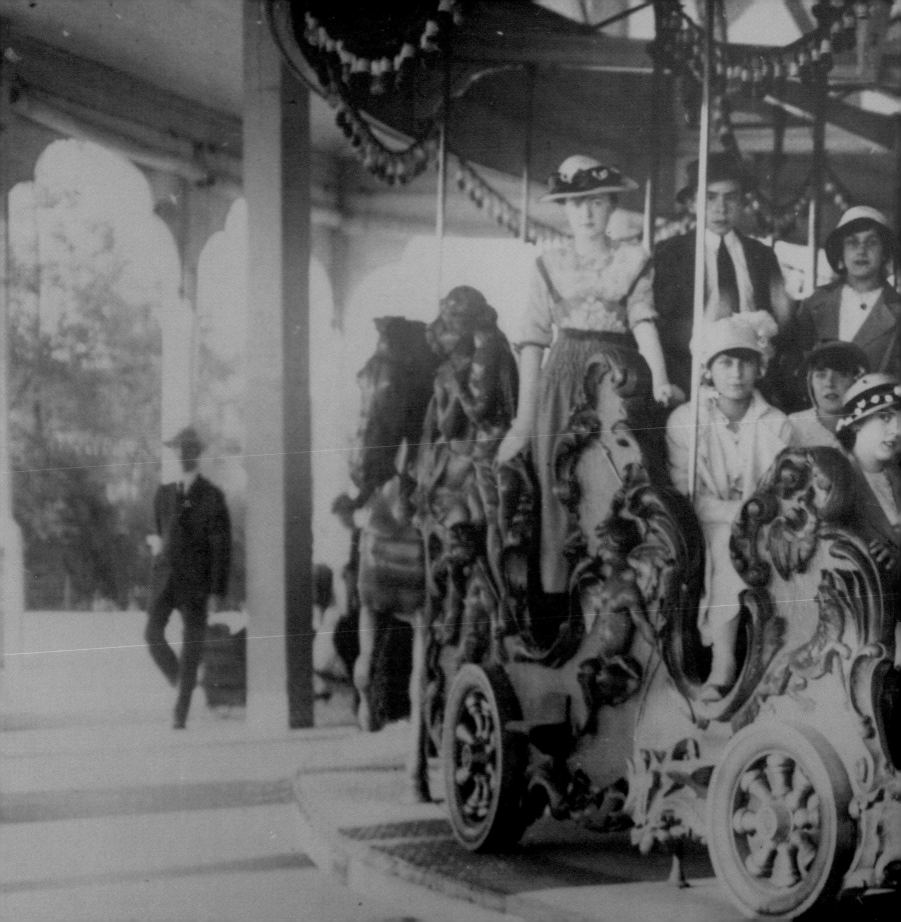

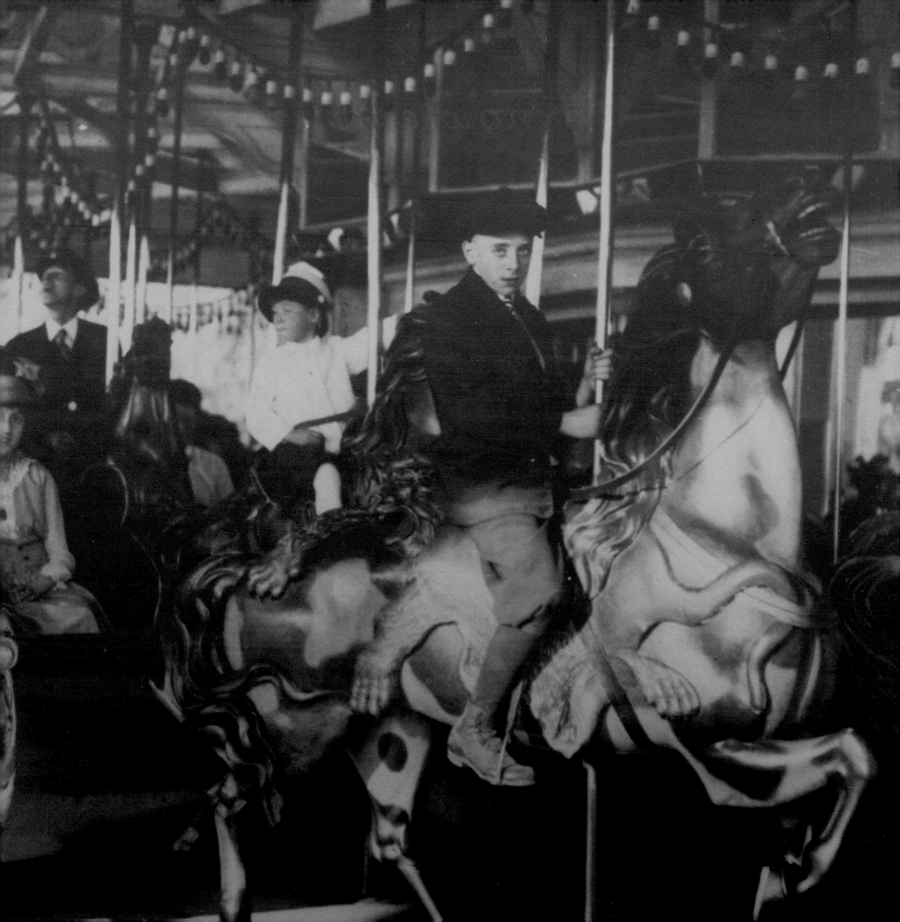

Acknowledgments

One of the great joys of creating this book was the opportunity that it offered to work with dozens of people who enthusiastically shared with me their personal memories, photographs, and collections of the carousel world. This book would not exist without their help, encouragement, and expertise. ❧ I would like to give my heartfelt thanks to the following: my parents, Maurice and Nina Fraley, for the stream of information forwarded to me and for their searches through endless boxes and slide trays for just the right images; Rol and Jo Summit, without whose continued encouragement and vast number of cross-country phone calls and packages, this project would still be "in the works"; Barbara Fahs Charles for contributing important photographic work along with her extensive knowledge, and for her willingness to meet me in the middle; Marion Dentzel for allowing me to rummage through her archives and set up a photo studio in her living room; Gary and Bonnie Wolf for more great inspiration; Willie Looff Taucher for graciously opening her home and family album to yet another carousel person; David Shayt at the Smithsonian Institution for his time and efforts in locating very valuable material; John and Jan Davis for digging through boxes and coming up with some great photographs; Charles Rutter for sharing memories of his work with his grandfather at the Philadelphia Toboggan Company

PRECEDING PAGES: A GROUP OF RIDERS POSES
ABOARD THE THREE-SEATER "LOVERS" CHARIOT ON THE
PHILADELPHIA TOBOGGAN COMPANY CAROUSEL AT
RIVERVIEW PARK IN CHICAGO. C. 1915.
PHOTO: COURTESY OF CHICAGO HISTORICAL SOCIETY.

and the Dentzel Company; Thomas Rebbie of Philadelphia Toboggan Coasters, Inc., for opening up his archives; Elizabeth Brick at the Herschell Carrousel Factory Museum, Geoff Weedon, Marguerite Cherny, and David Wynn at Knoebels Grove, Robert Muller and Merrick Price at Sea Breeze Park, Bob Ott and Alison Ruby for their contributions of very valuable photographs and information; Rosa Ragan, Will Morton, Gerry Holzman, Bill Finkenstein, and Joe Leonard for taking the time to tell us their stories; and to Carol Bialkowski for her insightful interviews. ❧ I would also like to thank John and Cathy Daniel, Charlotte Dinger, the Freels Foundation, and Earl Corey for allowing the use of their carousel figures. ❧ The following are the photographers whose excellent work appears throughout the book: Jacques Cresaty, Richard Blair, Gary Sinick, Phil Bray, Maurice Fraley, Barbara Fahs Charles, and Bill Kane.

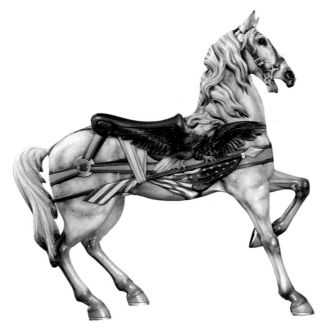

AN OUTSIDE-ROW DENTZEL HORSE, C. 1907,
SHOWING A FULL EAGLE AND AN AMERICAN FLAG.
FREELS FOUNDATION COLLECTION.

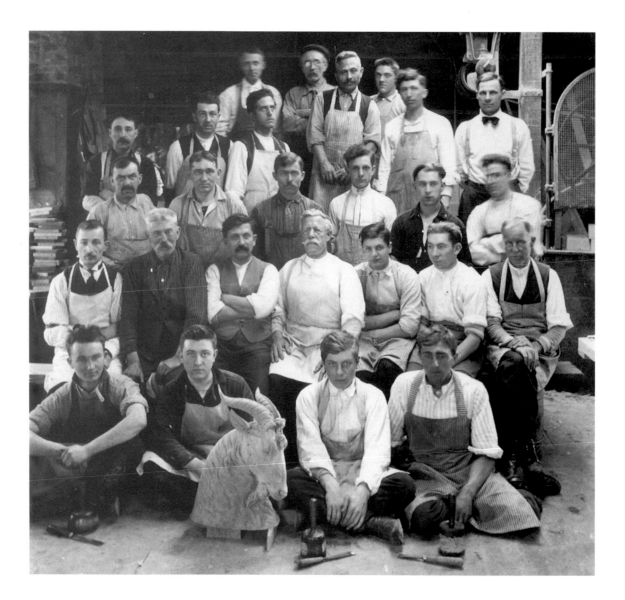

THE IMMIGRANT FACES OF THE CARVING SHOP AT THE
HERSCHELL-SPILLMAN COMPANY IN 1915.
PHOTO: COURTESY OF HERSCHEL- CARROUSEL FACTORY MUSEUM.

Foreword

Riding a carousel is a simple pleasure, a journey back to our childhood. Our horse, though made of wood, is a gallant and trustworthy steed. He jumps and spins to the band organ's lilting tunes, then brings us safely home again. We are exhilarated and amused and, for most of us, the ride ends. But for those who study the history and development of the American carousel, the ride has only begun. Our wooden horse can take us on a journey to a golden era during turn-of-the-century America and, on its carved wooden sides, we can read a chapter in the story of something we call "The American Spirit." ❧ *The American carousel is a unique combination of handcraft and machinery. On its platforms ride the products of the woodcarver's skill, hand-carved artwork of great delicacy and beauty. Yet, behind the ornate facades, the panels and mirrors surrounding its great center pole, are the motors and gears of an Industrial Revolution that turned craftsmen into salesmen and artists into engineers. Turn down the volume of the carousel organ and you can hear the music of gears and the pulsating sounds of the motor. The carousel was built as a machine. What provided the fantasy and sheltered a few dozen craftsmen from the crush of industrialization, allowing them to continue to practice their trade, was the amusement industry's continuing need to have both carvings that dazzled the eye, and technology that added thrills.* ❧ *While the factories of a growing America developed the duplicating capacity of "production lines" and wood turned to steel in so many of their products, the carvers in the woodworking shops of the carousel industry were allowed a great deal of artistic freedom. The ride imposed restrictions on width and length, and certain basic body styles were agreed upon, but ornamentation of the horses' saddles and blankets was often left for the carvers to invent. Artists carved what they felt, and the sides of wooden animals became the pages in a book. It was a book written, primarily, by immigrants who joined the tidal wave arriving on America's shores between 1860 and 1914. Their message tells us something of what it was like to become an American.* ❧ *What led twenty-five million Europeans to leave their homes, putting their lives in jeopardy on a difficult journey to a destination that was more a myth than a reality? Some were the poor, looking for a better life. The Irish fled starvation as the Great Potato Famine devastated the population of Ireland. Some came as political and religious refugees, fleeing failed revolutions and pogroms. From such a variety of reasons can we find one deep, underlying common need? Emma Lazarus expressed such a sentiment when she gave voice to the Statue of Liberty in 1883, asking Europe to send forth its "huddled masses yearning to breathe free." The promise of freedom was America's most powerful lure. The immigrants came to forge new ways from old traditions and to start a life reborn in freedom. The carousel carvers left us enduring symbols of what coming to America meant to so many millions.* ❧ *Their message can be read in the carved lines of our carousel horse. He pushes forward, his legs stretching out in a wild gallop. His head is flung upward and his mane flows wildly as if in a wind blowing across an open prairie. Everything about him speaks of an animal set free. In Europe his counterpart rides in a constrained circle, each horse like the other, and all mirroring the pose of the child's rocking horse from which his carver drew inspiration. There is little freedom to run on his carousel; he rides under a tight rein.* ❧ *We notice this freedom of movement, so eloquently expressed in the body of the horse, before saddle carvings catch our attention, but it is in these areas of detailed decoration where the carver has the greatest freedom of expression. It is here that we find an almost overwhelming profu-*

sion of Americana. Some elements of European tradition remained. There were armored knights, their shields replete with heraldic lions. Cherubs and angels were a favorite subject and drapery was often embroidered with fleurs-de-lys or carved to resemble tapestry. But as time passed, drapery became an American flag, and the knight could as easily be a cowboy, or even Teddy Roosevelt on his way up San Juan Hill. Marcus Charles Illions, born in Lithuania, carved a portrait of Lincoln on the side of an armored horse. Daniel Müller immigrated from Germany with his family in 1882. The Wild West frontier fired the imagination of this ten-year-old boy, for years later, as a mature, gifted artist, he created very realistic U.S. Cavalry horses riding on some of the most beautiful carousels ever made. Columbia, the goddess-like personification of the United States whose form or face graced silver coins and statehouses, also sat in splendor on the sides of chariots and looked out over the midway's crowds from the rounding boards on the carousel's upper rim. ∾ Twelve major carving companies dominated the carousel industry in its most productive years between 1880 and 1918. Competing for contracts in the flourishing amusement business, the company owners and the carvers who created for them developed a keen sense of what was currently of interest to the American public. The art of the carousel was not an exhibition in museum halls or national galleries. It was a living art, tested by the nickels and dimes of a public who flocked to trolley parks, resorts, and small town fairs all across the country. If it failed to give substance to common beliefs and ambitions, and to hopes that persevered in spite of the drab realities faced in the ghettos and tenements that were the immigrants' most common experience, then it failed at the ticket booths. ∾ The carousel ride did not fail. It represents the success of a group of primarily immigrant craftsmen, artists, and entrepreneurs in the exercise of one of America's most valued institutions, the free enterprise system. If the streets of America were not paved with gold, the manes and trappings of its carousel horses were, shimmering with the promise of a ride to prosperity and freedom. ❧ The family amusement park, such an important element in the development of the carousel ride, has slid into near oblivion. Like the family store on the corner crushed by the supermarket chains, the smaller, local parks have been dwarfed by corporate theme parks and pressured by skyrocketing insurance and labor costs, and by a population enamored of the kind of passive entertainment offered by television and spectator sports. Operating carousels, which once numbered in the thousands, now count fewer than two hundred. Riding the carousel was once a common experience shared by a good portion of America's youngsters. For the city's children, the amusement park was a trolley ride away. In the farming communities of the mountain states and Midwest, families could travel to the county seat at fair time and ride the carnival carousel for a nickel. But as the rides dropped from public view, an amazing phenomenon took place. Carousels and what they represented were not forgotten. Organizations sprang up filled with enthusiasm for history and restoration techniques. Books were published and study grants were awarded. Museums exhibited carousel art as a legitimate segment of our national heritage, and arguments ensued over "Folk Art" and "Fine Art" labels. Communities banded together and launched crusades to save operating carousels. ❧ Is this second stage in the history of the carousel a fad that will fade once it has temporarily relieved our boredom? Ask the thousands of people who, sometimes in embarrassment, admit that they always want to ride on one whenever they have an opportunity. Ask the hundreds of thousands who would jump at the chance to spend a few minutes whirling on a carousel; then just look at their faces, reflecting a dream that still lives on. It is a ride that never ends.

Nina Fraley

Preface

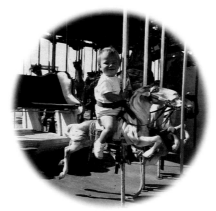

The carousel business is strange. It's not a subject that you can just take a course in, like accounting, marketing, or computer programming. There are no college degrees, no professors, no textbooks. High school guidance counselors don't talk about it as a career option. It's not listed in those books that describe the hundreds of different jobs in existence. Nor is it posted in the Help Wanted section of the local newspaper.

Nevertheless, I found myself in the carousel business seventeen years ago. It wasn't a conscious decision; it just happened. But when I piece together the memories of my childhood experiences, it's no wonder I'm in this business. In reality, I spent most of my life preparing for this career without really knowing it. *Growing up in Seattle in the 1950s, I led a somewhat unusual life (although I didn't think so at the time). But when I stop to compare it with the lifestyles of my grammar school friends, I can't deny that it was different. After all, I was the only kid on the block with a grandfather who owned an amusement park.* *Like any child who has an amusement park in the family, I took advantage of the privileges that go along with that distinction—going on the rides for free, eating all the hot dogs and popcorn I wanted—things that most kids only fantasize*

THE AUTHOR TAKES HIS FIRST RIDE ON THE CAROUSEL
AT HIS GRANDFATHER'S PARK IN SEATTLE, WASHINGTON.

1 5

about. That amusement park played a very special role in my childhood until 1961, the year the city decided to build a small amusement park in the downtown area, forcing my grandfather to close Playland. Vacating the park was not an easy job. It wasn't as if we could simply put the rides in boxes and keep them in storage; so they were disassembled and sold—all but the carousel, which my parents inherited after my grandfather lost his battle with cancer. ❧ *A year later we moved south, to my father's hometown of Berkeley, California, with a carousel full of animals in tow. Our new home was a bit unusual, even for California. At least a dozen carousel animals were hanging around the house at any one time, lounging in the living room, standing guard in the bedroom, looking over our shoulders when we ate dinner.* ❧ *The carousel figures that didn't fit in our house took up residence in the art gallery that my parents owned. Little by little, they began to work on some of the more ornate creatures, stripping off the old paint, repairing any damage, and putting on a shiny new coat. Eventually they sold some of the figures, then bought others. By 1969, working with carousel "art" was their full-time occupation. As my parents became more deeply involved in the business and history of carousel animals, they met other people who shared their interest. In the early 1970s they became two of the first members of the National Carousel Association.* ❧ *I, on the other hand, had no interest in pursuing a career in carousel animals. My interest in Northwest Coast Indian art led me to learn about woodcarving. When I was twenty-three I spent a year in the wilds of Washington as an apprentice to woodcarver Ernest Jenner. Ernie was an excellent carver and a very nice guy, but not much of a teacher. My first carving assignment was to reproduce the detail at the top of an old column for a Seattle brewery. He gave me a sample of what it was supposed to look like, put a block of wood in front of me, and said, "Make another one." So I did, or at least I attempted to. But I didn't do a very good job. In time, however, I did pick up the basics of woodcarving.*

After a year in Washington I came back to California and stepped into the world of carousels. I received my first taste of the business by restoring some of the animals in my parents' gallery. When things were slow, I worked on figures brought in by other collectors in a little studio that I had set up in the corner of the shop. Through word of mouth, the demand for my restoration work grew, and it wasn't long before that corner was too small. By 1979 there was enough work for me to open my own restoration studio in Oakland. For the first year I worked alone, doing all of the woodcarving, painting, and paperwork. As the business continued to expand, I hired another woodcarver, then a painter and a bookkeeper. The extra hands enabled me to put the studio on automatic pilot and take time off to work on my first book. The inspiration for The Carousel Animal *came about when I was visiting friends in Massachusetts who happen to be carousel animal enthusiasts. As we were looking at a picture book about the history of the jukebox, one of us asked the rhetorical question, "Wouldn't it be great if there was a book like this about carousel animals?" The light bulb went on. I returned home the following week and started working on the book. Nine months later the finished product was in print.* With that first book finished, I was free to concentrate on the restoration business. As carousel animals grew in popularity, so did the demand for restoration work. Before long, bus loads of tourists were beating a path to the front door, eager to find out about this unusual art form and to relive wonderful childhood memories of whirling effortlessly on a mighty steed. Then, ten years to the day after deciding to write the first book, as I was celebrating Christmas with the same friends in Massachusetts, we realized that it was time for a new book and that it should be about the talented people who created carousels. So here is a look at the remarkable craftsmen and artists who produced the enduring and endearing art that we have come to love, respect, and cherish.*

CAROUSEL: THE CONCEPT

❁ ❁ ❁ ❁ ❁ ❁ ❁ ❁ ❁ ❁ ❁ ❁ ❁ ❁ ❁ ❁ ❁ ❁ ❁

CHAPTER 1

In England, they've been called roundabouts and gallopers; in France, carrousels and manèges de chevaux de bois; in Germany, karussell; and in America, whirligigs, flying horses, and merry-go-rounds. Carousels have been known by many names. Yet no one knows exactly where or when the first carousel-like spinning ride came into being. A Byzantine relief dating around A.D. 500 shows acrobats, jugglers, and bears watching riders swing in baskets tied to a pole. A manuscript from 1620 describes a horizontal "cart wheel" fastened with little seats. An early seventeenth-century painting depicts two variations of Turkish carousels, as well as a Ferris wheel, swings, and other rides.

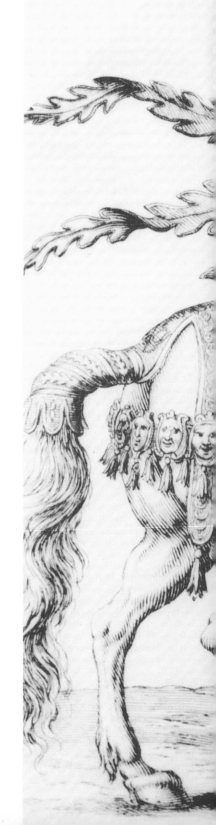

THE DECORATIONS FOUND ON THE HORSES DURING THE PAGEANTRY OF GRAND EVENTS WENT ON TO INSPIRE MANY CAROUSEL MAKERS SEVERAL CENTURIES LATER.

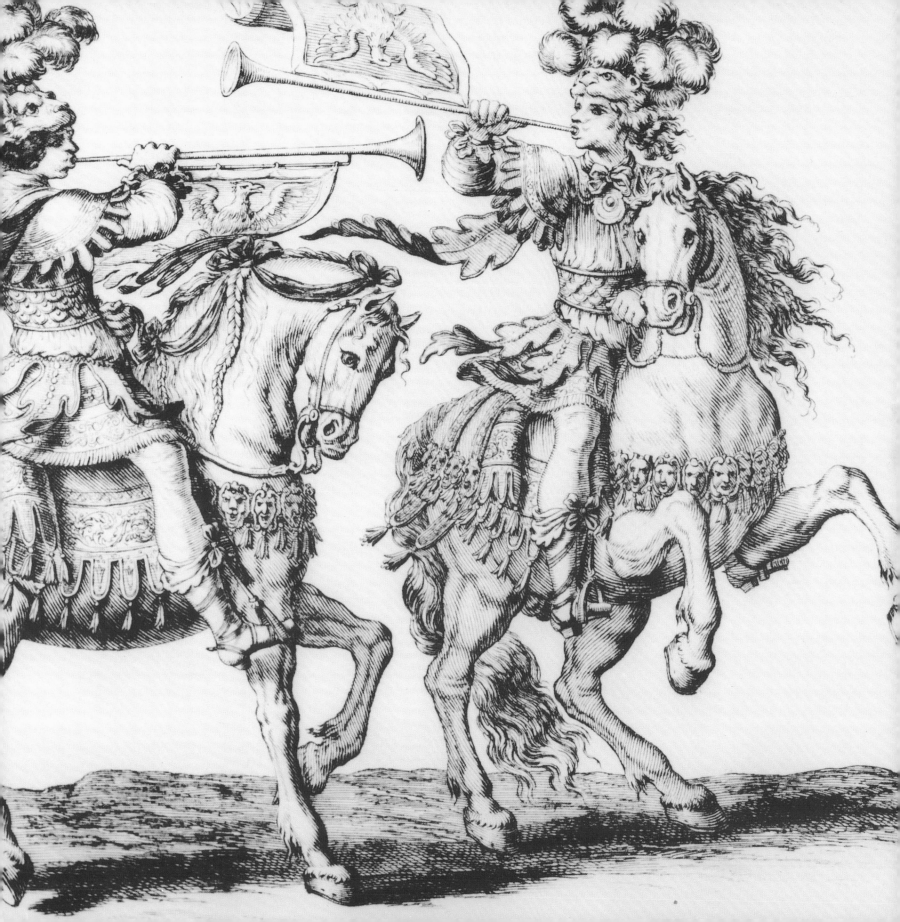

Although the origin of the carousel itself is unknown, the origin of the word *is* known. It can be traced to a serious contest of horsemanship called *carosello* (meaning "little war" in Italian), played in Arabia and Turkey during the twelfth century. The ground rules were simple. Delicate clay balls filled with perfumed water were deftly tossed from one moving rider to another. The object of the game was to catch the fragile balls and, in doing so, avoid the unmanly stench of defeat.

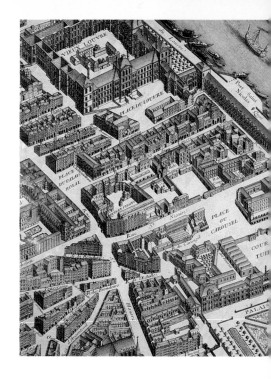

At about the time that Columbus landed in America, a form of the game found its way to the court of the French monarch, Charles VIII. The French called it *carousel* and transformed it into a magnificent event of pomp and pageantry. *Le Grand Carousel*, the most famous and lavish of all, was planned by Louis XIV in 1662 to impress his teenage mistress, Louise de la Vallière. This great spectacle, which was attended by thousands, took place in the square between the Tuileries gardens and the Louvre. Today, this area of Paris is still called the Place du Carousel. And the Arc du Carousel remains a tourist attraction.

The French added several other games to the *carousel,* including the sport of ring piercing once played by the ancient Moors. It called for a steady hand, superb horsemanship, and a sharp eye, for the object of the contest was to lance a small ring with a sword while riding at full speed. The ring was suspended by brightly colored ribbons hung from the limb of a tree or between two posts. When pierced, the ring slid down the shaft of the sword and a stream of ribbons fluttered in the breeze.

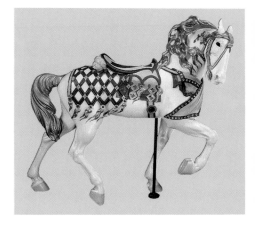

In the late seventeenth century, young French noblemen trained for this game by lancing rings while riding legless wooden "horses" attached to a rotating platform. (Thus, the carousel as we know it, and its game of "catching the brass ring," was born.) The practice machine quickly evolved into a popular form of entertainment among other members of the court, including women and children. And, as local craftsmen began building their own versions of this relatively simple piece of equipment, they discovered that the demand wasn't limited to nobility: the carousel appealed to the aristocracy and peasants alike.

By 1800 the popularity of this new type of public entertainment had spread throughout Europe. However, the size and weight of the carousel were limited by its power source, which, until just after midcentury, was supplied by horse, mule, or man.

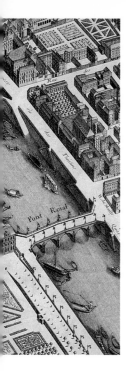

Although there are reports of the use of steam power in connection with a round-about as early as 1863, it was another three years before an engineer named Frederick Savage effectively combined the two. Even though Savage's roundabouts were taking the fairs of Europe by storm, the idea of steam-powered carousels would not reach the United States for another fifteen years.

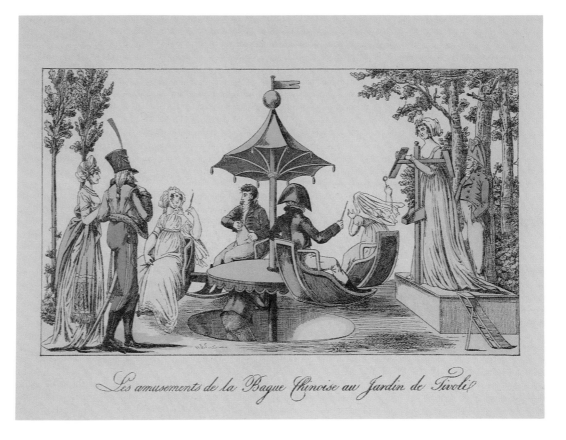

Les amusements de la Bague Chinoise au Jardin de Tivoli

ABOVE: THE TURGOT MAP OF PARIS SHOWING THE PLACE DU CAROUSEL WHERE LOUIS XIV HELD HIS GRAND TOURNAMENT IN 1662. NEW YORK PUBLIC LIBRARY, MAP ROOM.

LEFT: MARCUS CHARLES ILLIONS WAS ONE OF THE CARVERS TO BE INFLUENCED BY THE BEAUTIFULLY DECORATED HORSES OF THE FRENCH COURT. THIS OUTSIDE-ROW STANDER, C. 1912, IS CERTAINLY ONE OF THOSE FIGURES. COLLECTION OF CHARLOTTE DINGER.

RIGHT: THE FRENCH ARISTOCRACY WAS THE FIRST GROUP TO USE THE CAROUSEL PRACTICE MACHINE FOR PURE ENTERTAINMENT. SEVERAL MEMBERS OF THE COURT ARE SHOWN HERE TRYING TO SPEAR THE BRASS RING ON AN EARLY CAROUSEL IN THE TUILERIES GARDENS. PHOTO: COURTESY OF NEW YORK PUBLIC LIBRARY PICTURE COLLECTION.

FREDERICK SAVAGE

Born in 1828, in the English village of Hevinghas, Frederick Savage had grown up during the height of the Industrial Revolution. He studied the mechanics of steam power and eventually opened a small machine shop in the town of King's Lynn. Initially he created farm equipment, but in 1865, he made a trip to the nearby Aylsham Fair where he saw Sidney George Soames's "Steam Circus," a collection of amusement devices that ran on steam power. Soames's device fascinated Savage, not because he cared about what it did, but because he knew he could build a better one.

Within a year Savage rigged one of his engines to run an all-bicycle carousel, or "velocipede," as it was known. It was an instant success. Patents followed patents for this agricultural engineer turned amusement entrepreneur. His invention of the overhead cranking devices allowed his English gallopers to mimic the motion of an actual horse. The same design for the gears and cranks that made his animals go up and down are used on carousels today.

Frederick Savage's ingenuity made him a pioneer in carousel engineering. For his inspired contributions, he can truly be thanked for helping the world to turn a little bit faster.

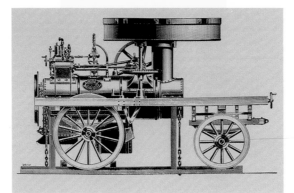

INVENTED AND MANUFACTURED BY FREDERICK SAVAGE,
THE CENTER TRUCK WAS A PORTABLE STEAM ENGINE USED
TO TURN — "A TRAVELING CAROUSEL." PHOTO: COURTESY OF
GEOFF WEEDON.

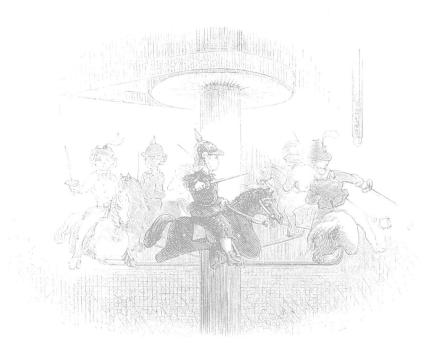

RIGHT: As the carousel spread to the general public it took on the form of a simple machine filled with legless horses. These young riders were properly dressed for the occasion. Photo: courtesy of New York Public Library Picture Collection.

BELOW: In Parisian life during the 1850s, a day in the park was incomplete without a ride on the carousel. Photo: courtesy of New York Public Library Picture Collection.

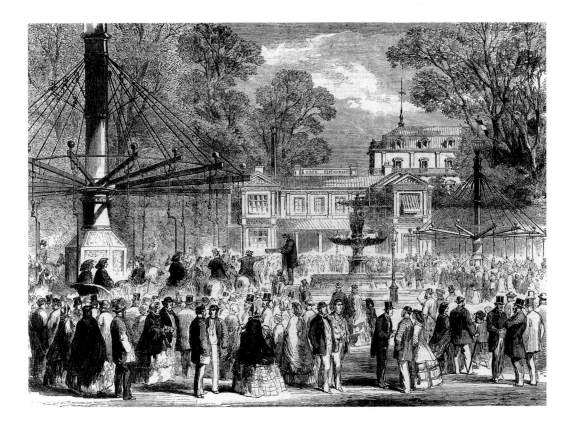

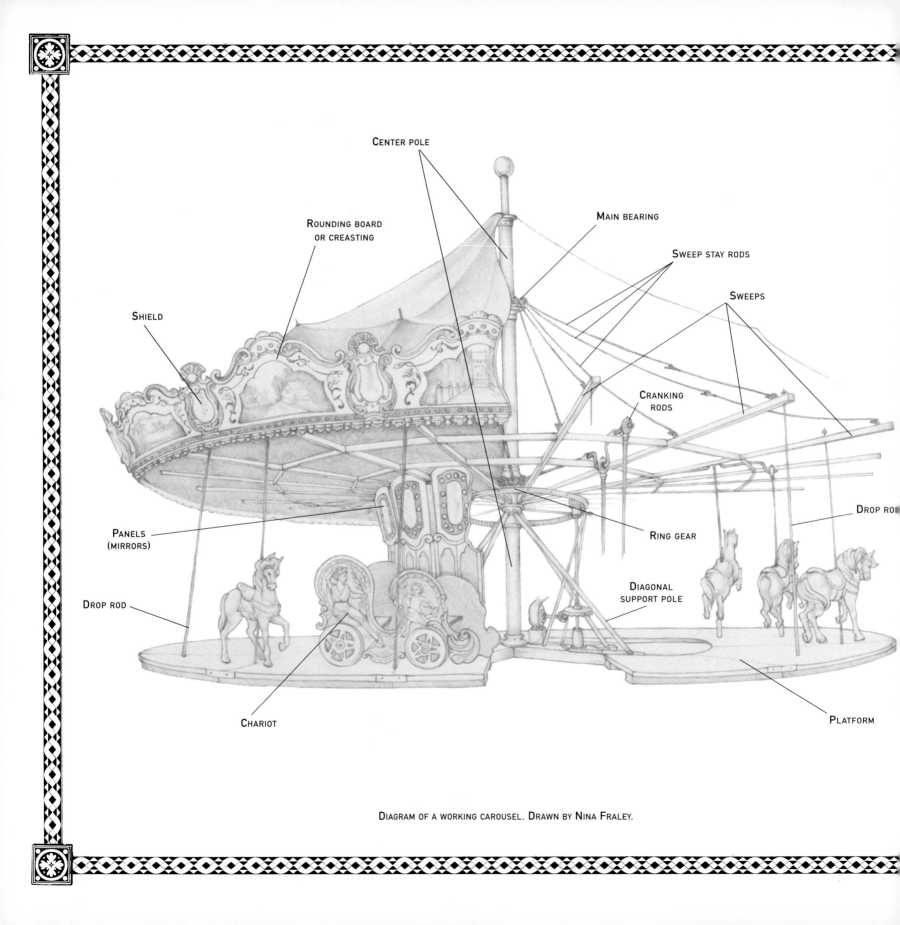

CENTER POLE

ROUNDING BOARD
OR CREASTING

MAIN BEARING

SWEEP STAY RODS

SWEEPS

SHIELD

CRANKING
RODS

PANELS
(MIRRORS)

RING GEAR

DROP ROD

DROP ROD

DIAGONAL
SUPPORT POLE

CHARIOT

PLATFORM

DIAGRAM OF A WORKING CAROUSEL. DRAWN BY NINA FRALEY.

HOW IT WORKS

The mechanics of the carousel have taken 1500 years to evolve from a basket spinning around a pole on the end of a rope to the carousel as it is known today, yet the inner workings of this machine are still relatively simple. The one thing that has not changed since medieval times is the center pole. Like the hub of a wheel, this part of the carousel is essential and has always remained constant.

The modern carousel is suspended from cables attached to the top of the center pole. These cables are connected to a series of spokes (or sweeps) that extend outward over the platform from the center. The sweeps hold up the platform with rods, which pass through both the sweeps and the platform and are bolted on each end (these rods are often covered with brass). This form of support allows the platform to "float" above the ground, giving the riders a wonderfully smooth ride. The turn of the carousel then becomes similar to that of a pie tin spinning on the end of a juggler's stick.

The up and down motion of the animals is produced by a simple set of gears and cranks. The internal ring gear is like a large, thin, stationary donut with a continuous set of teeth. The crank that makes an individual row of animals go up and down has a round gear the size of a dinner plate attached to one end. This end gear fits snugly into the ring gear, as in an egg beater, and the crank then turns as the carousel goes around. You don't usually see these gears on a carousel because they are hidden just behind the inner panels covering the center of the machine.

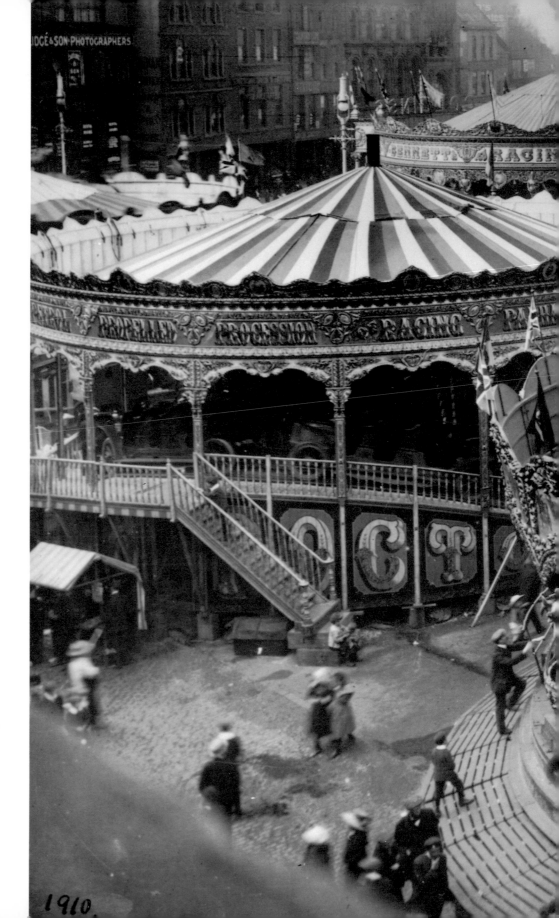

The Nottingham Goose Fair started out in the early 1800s as exactly that, a goose fair where various fowl were bartered for, bought, and sold. Over the years it took on a distinctly different look, becoming more carnival than bird show. By 1910, when this scene was taken, it had become one of England's largest fairs and was dominated by the steam-powered roundabout. Photo: courtesy of Geoff Weedon.

26

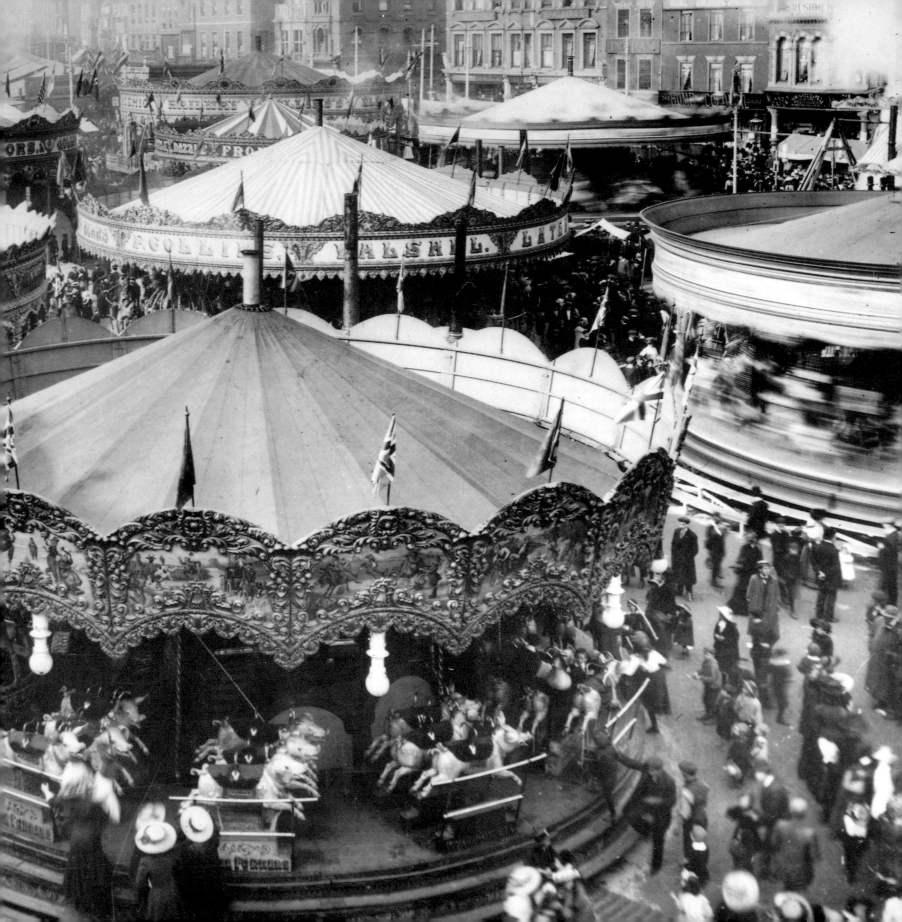

COMING TO AMERICA

❖❖❖❖❖❖❖❖❖❖❖❖❖❖❖❖❖

CHAPTER 2

Upon *landing in this new country,*
immigrants saw their dream of a land of plenty quickly
fade in the harsh light of reality. Long work hours,
cramped living spaces, and low wages dampened the
spirits of these new would-be citizens. Skills that may have
been useful in a different culture were now of little help in
providing for a family. Although jobs were plentiful, they
required little or no expertise.

Only the most resourceful were able to turn their old
world abilities into a viable form of employment. Among
this enterprising group was a young man of twenty named

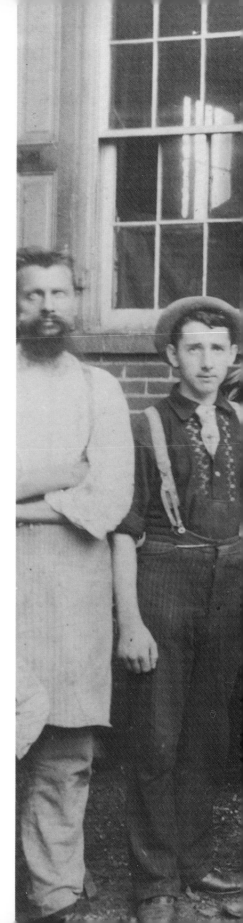

The Dentzel shop in 1889. Gustav Dentzel is on the far right; second from the left is Daniel Müller, while his brother Alfred and father, John, are second and third from the right in the middle row. Photo: courtesy of Robert Muller.

28

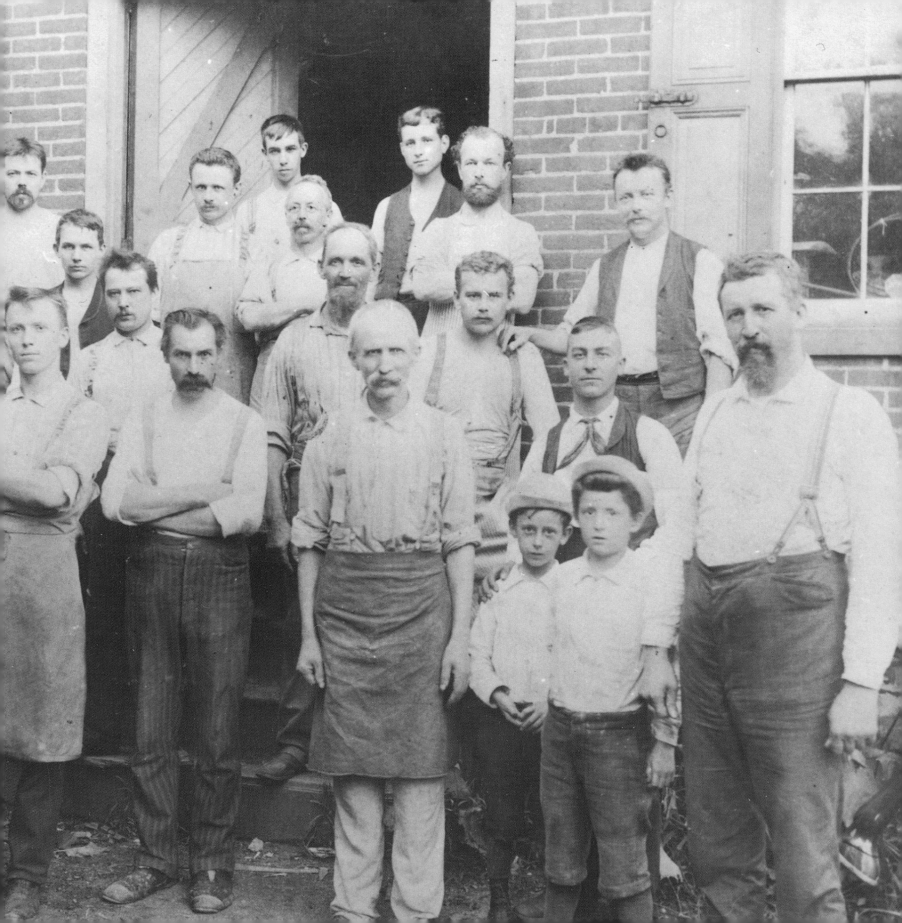

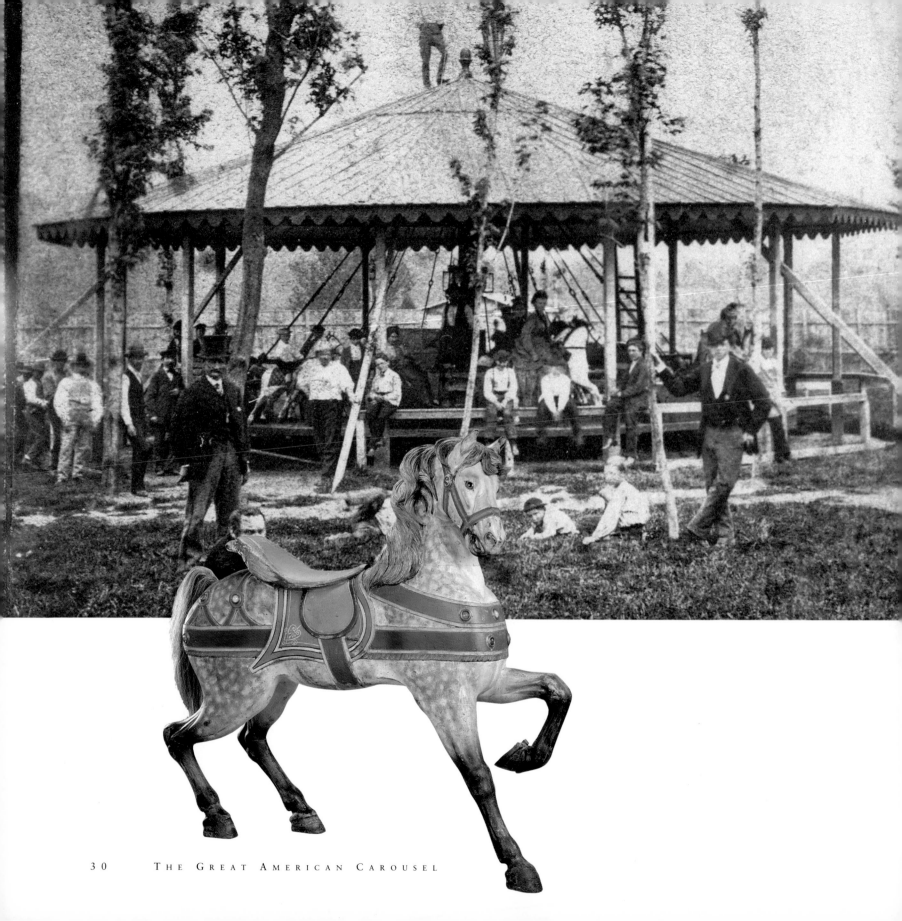

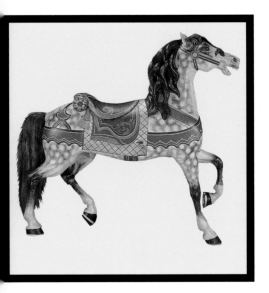

Gustav Dentzel. After his arrival rom Kreuznach, Germany, Gustav settled in Philadelphia, where he promptly opened a cabinet-making shop. Dentzel brought not only his skills as an expert carver and craftsman, but also a heritage deeply rooted in the lore of the carousel. Gustav's father, Michael Dentzel, had built and operated several machines in Germany.

By 1867, when Gustav decided to try his hand at the carousel business and build his own machine, carousels had already been established. After successfully operating the carousel, first at an amusement center in Philadelphia and then in Atlantic City, Dentzel decided to take the carousel on the road. For the next five years he traveled throughout the East, making a living by selling tickets to his all-horse "carroussell." With constant travel and poor living conditions as a given, it was not an easy life, although Dentzel did manage to support his family and even to build up a small savings. As business increased he hired a crew to operate his first carousel while he went back to Philadelphia to construct more machines.

Eventually a promoter offered to buy one of his carousels. Realizing that production might be easier than operation, Dentzel accepted the offer and returned to Philadelphia to build carousels full time. Despite this change, the majority of Dentzel's income was still derived from the operation of his machines, but that was soon to change.

By 1876, other companies began to appear, perhaps inspired by Dentzel's success or possibly by an increasing fascination for this new type of amusement. Over the next twenty years, dozens of manufacturers sprang up around the country. Some were official carousel factories such as Norman & Evans, The American Merry-Go-Round & Novelty Company, and The Bungarz Steam Wagon & Carrousele Works, while other carousels came from the backyards of would-be entrepreneurs who created crude but functional rides out of whatever wood was available.

The fragmented records that remain from most of these carousel makers show a great deal of enthusiasm but very little result. Although in industry publications such as *Billboard* many companies claimed to be turning out carousels on a weekly basis and boasted that orders were pouring in, their output rarely exceeded a few per year. Only the most creative, talented, and fortunate of these makers lasted more than a couple of years in this competitive business. Besides Dentzel, three others were able to sustain momentum during the early years. Both Charles Dare and Charles Looff opened shops in New York City, while Allan Herschell and his partner, James Armitage, transformed their successful machine shop in

DARE'S HORSES ARE HIGHLY PRIZED NOT ONLY BY CAROUSEL COLLECTORS BUT BY MARBLE COLLECTORS WHO CLAIM THAT THE LARGE SULFITE MARBLES HE USED FOR THE EYES OF HIS HORSES ARE QUITE VALUABLE. PHOTO: COURTESY OF MAURICE FRALEY.

North Tonawanda, New York, into an even more successful carousel company.

Charles Looff was one of the talented and tenacious immigrants who turned his dream of creating a better life into a reality. His first carousel, made in 1876, was constructed from scraps gathered at the furniture company were he worked. Once completed, he installed it in a popular beach pavilion at a newly developed district of New York City called Coney Island, soon to become the most celebrated amusement park in the country. The ride sported a variety of menagerie animals, including camels, zebras, and ostriches, along with the traditional horses.

Soon after producing this first machine, Looff opened his own shop in Brooklyn where he constructed a second carousel. This more refined effort was installed at Feltman's restaurant complex at Coney Island around 1880. Struck by entrepreneurial inspiration, Looff built his first three carousels entirely by himself; the third appeared at Young's Pier in Atlantic City, New Jersey.

Looff leaned toward a more fanciful design in both his carousels and the buildings that housed them. Later, he added glass jewels and beveled mirrors to the trappings, created animated leg positions for his horses, and carved wild manes, often using gold leaf. By adding electric lights to the carousel and colored glass in the windows of the building, he further enhanced the highly decorative nature of the animals.

As Looff was putting the finishing touches on his second machine, Charles Dare was transforming his rocking horse and amusement device company into the New York Carousal Manufacturing Company, later renamed the Charles W. Dare Company. Most of the menagerie of wooden animals that came from this shop have been lost over the past ninety years.

Whether by intent or accident, Dare's relatively simple figures proved easier to transport than the larger animals produced by

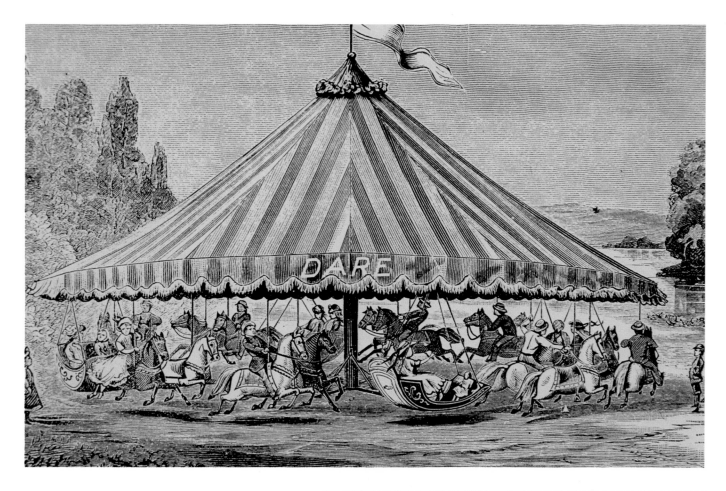

ABOVE: CHARLES DARE'S SIMPLY DESIGNED CAROUSELS WERE CREATED SPECIFICALLY FOR USE IN TRAVELING FAIRS AND CARNIVALS. THIS ARTIST'S INTERPRETATION OF A DARE MACHINE WAS TAKEN FROM AN EARLY ISSUE OF BILLBOARD MAGAZINE IN WHICH DARE FREQUENTLY ADVERTISED. COURTESY OF NEW YORK PUBLIC LIBRARY.

RIGHT: CHARLES LOOFF STANDS BY HIS FIRST CAROUSEL, WHICH HE INSTALLED AT CONEY ISLAND, NEW YORK, IN 1876. PHOTO: WILLIE LOOFF TAUCHER.

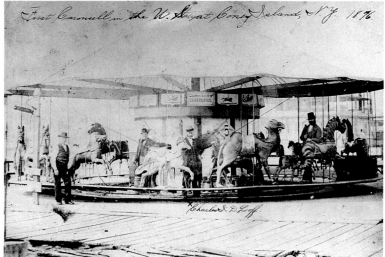

WHAT'S IN A WORD?

For centuries the word "carousel" (derived from the Italian word carosello, *meaning "little war") meant a tournament based on horsemanship and skill with a sword or lance. Since the days of those tournaments the meaning has continued to change, until it has become associated with almost anything that revolves, including round slide trays, baggage claim machines, and changers for CD players. But the most common use is for the large turning machine filled with wooden animals that we are all familiar with. Whether they are called flying horses, steam riding galleries, merry-go-rounds, or carousels, they are all the same machine. The number of animals varies as do the mechanics of the ride, but the names are interchangeable.*

Just as the meaning of the word has evolved, the spelling has varied as much as possible. The original French word was carousel, *but carousel companies have added letters to create words such as Gustav Dentzel's original name, Steam and Horsepower Caroussell Builder, or Solomon Stein and Harry Goldstein's Artistic Carousel Manufacturing Company. Charles Looff called his machines "carroussels," C. W. Dare used "carousal," while Charles W. Parker turned the word into "Carry-us-all." Since there is really no correct spelling, the spelling chosen here is the simplest: one "r," one "s," and one "l."*

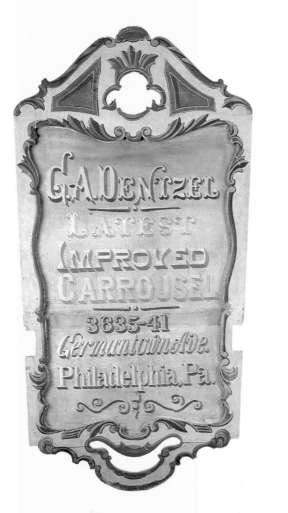 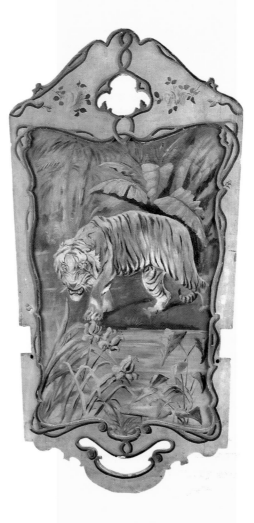

The rounding boards and panels not only enhanced the adventure of riding a carousel but also let the patrons know who had made it in case they wanted one of their own.

Dentzell and Loof. They became the perfect ride for traveling circuses and carnivals. Unfortunately, most traveling carousels were eventually abandoned in old barns or simply tossed onto scrap heaps when they became too costly to maintain or when a traveling show went out of business. The unique large marble eyes of the few figures by Dare that do remain set them apart from their imitators.

Aside from a few catalogs and some advertising, little more is known about Dare. Despite the initial success of Dare's company, the economic depression of the late 1890s took its toll, and by 1900 Dare was out of business. Although Dare's company did not continue operating into the following century, his influence as an innovator in the burgeoning world of carousels certainly did.

Allan Herschell must have been thinking of Dare's horse designs when he tried to convince his business partner, James Armitage, that there was a future in the amusement business. Having already established a successful steam engine and boiler company, Herschell was hard pressed to explain why they should try something as frivolous sounding as a "Steam Riding Gallery" carousel. In 1883, despite his skepticism, Armitage agreed to go along with Herschell's plan. Together, with Herschell's brother George, they began what was to become the longest lasting and most prolific of all the carousel manufacturing ventures.

A late entrant into the world of nineteenth-century carousel building was Charles W. Parker. Parker was enthralled with the success of the Armitage-Herschell Company and decided that there was a large demand for the traveling style of carousel in the Midwest, so in 1892, he opened up Parker Carnival Supply Company, later known as C. W. Parker Amusement Company. At first, Parker bought and refurbished Dare and Armitage-Herschell machines, reselling them under his company's name. Eventually he began creating his own figures, but it wasn't until after 1908 that Parker's designers came up with their own distinctive style.

By 1899, it became quite evident that no matter who made them, carousels were here to stay. Frederick Savage's idea of adding steam power, along with his jumping mechanism, came to the attention of U.S. carousel makers in the 1890s. With increased speed and more action, this "newfangled" device was a sure hit at any fair, carnival, or park. To the men making carousels it must have seemed that the heyday of popularity was upon them. In the span of thirty years the business had grown from a few crude carousels to a full-fledged, thriving business. Yet it was only the beginning.

OPPOSITE TOP: WHEN THE ARMITAGE-HERSCHELL COMPANY BEGAN CAROUSEL PRODUCTION, IT FOLLOWED IN THE FOOTSTEPS OF C. W. DARE BY PRODUCING TRAVELING CAROUSELS. BY THE EARLY 1890s THE ARMITAGE-HERSCHELL COMPANY HAD ADDED STEAM ENGINES TO ITS MACHINE AND CHANGED THE NAME OF ITS CAROUSELS TO "STEAM RIDING GALLERIES." PHOTO: COURTESY OF HERSCHELL CAROUSEL FACTORY MUSEUM.

OPPOSITE CENTER: IN THE LATE 1880s, COMPETITION AMONG THE CAROUSEL MAKERS INCREASED DRAMATICALLY. BUT, JUST AS TODAY, THERE WERE ALSO FOREIGN IMPORTS, SUCH AS THIS CAROUSEL BY FREDERICK SAVAGE, BROUGHT TO CONEY ISLAND BY F. E. BOSTOCK IN 1896. FROM SAVAGE'S MACHINES AMERICAN CAROUSEL MAKERS LEARNED OF STEAM AS A POWER SOURCE FOR CAROUSELS AND THE CRANKING DEVICE FOR MAKING THE ANIMALS "GALLOP." PHOTO: COURTESY OF STAPLES & CHARLES.

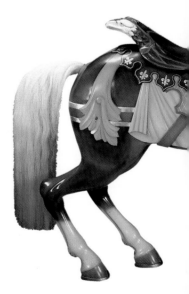

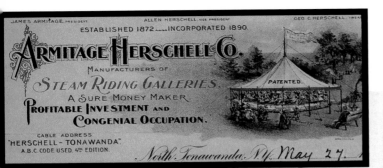

BOTTOM LEFT AND RIGHT: THE CLOSE COMPETITION AMONG
MANUFACTURERS WAS ALSO THE PRIME REASON FOR THE INCREASE
IN THE ORNATENESS OF THE TRAPPINGS. ALTHOUGH THE
DECORATIONS ON A HORSE WERE MINIMAL IN THE 1880S, FIFTEEN
YEARS LATER FOUND THAT THE MORE ADDED TO THE TRAPPINGS THE
BETTER. THE HORSE AT LEFT IS A DENTZEL, C. 1898, AND THE
HORSE AT RIGHT IS A LOOFF, C. 1899. COLLECTION OF JOHN AND
CATHY DANIEL (LEFT). COREY COLLECTION (RIGHT).

THE GOLDEN AGE ARRIVES

CHAPTER 3

1900 *brought with it the surging tide of the Industrial Revolution. Many of the innovations that had come about in the last thirty years were just finding their way into general public use. The three main ingredients that led to a renaissance of the amusement industry were the widespread use of electricity, mass transportation in the form of the trolley car and, later, the automobile, and leisure time. With more labor-saving devices creeping into the manufacturing sector, the country found itself using a new word—weekend.*

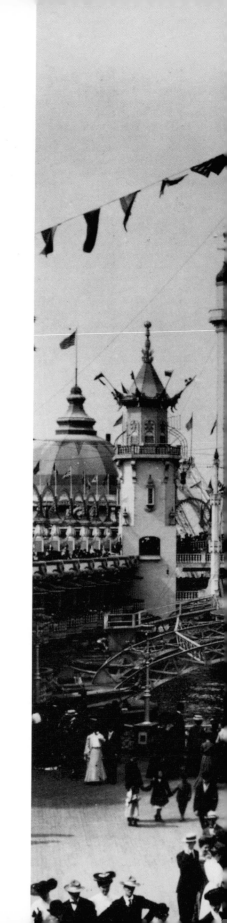

THE GRAND SCALE OF LUNA PARK AT CONEY ISLAND, NEW YORK, DURING THE HEIGHT OF ITS POPULARITY IN 1905. PHOTO: ADOLPH WITTEMANN, COURTESY OF MUSEUM OF THE CITY OF NEW YORK, THE LEONARD HASSAM BOGART COLLECTION.

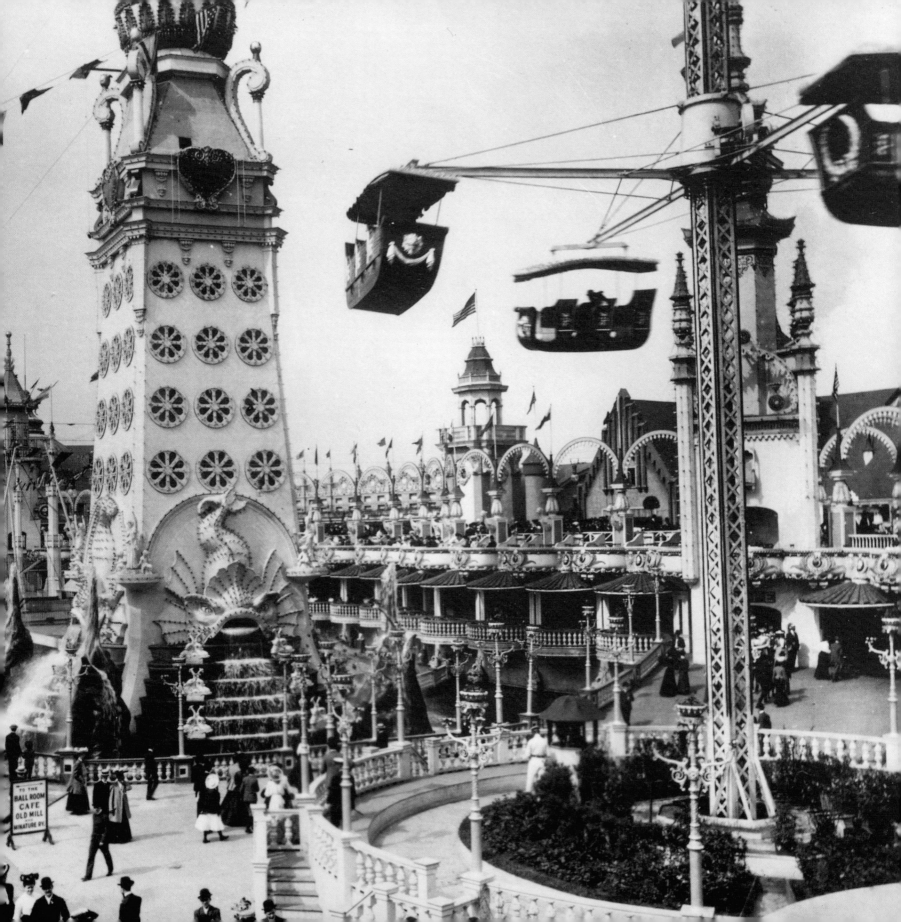

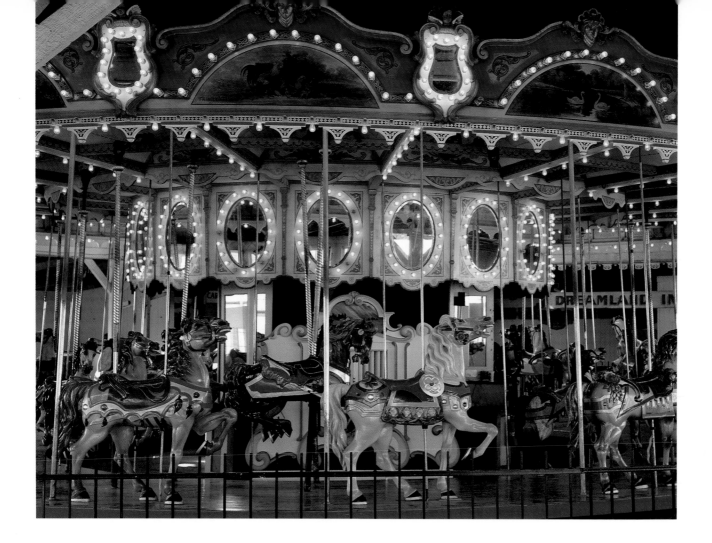

The question then became what to do with this newfound time. Many recently formed public and private transit associations had a grand idea. Since ridership dropped off on Saturdays and Sundays, why not give people somewhere to go and make some money at the same time? Looking toward the expansion of cities, and with government incentives in the form of land grants and right-of-ways, transit systems purchased or received vast tracks of land and laid track well beyond the city limits. The end of the line could be found in what were still fairly rural areas and so became the perfect place for a "trolley park."

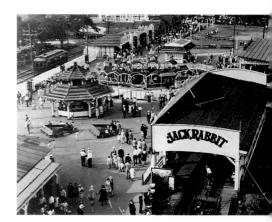

From 1898 to 1910, hundreds of trolley parks sprang up throughout the country. These parks ranged from picnic areas with a few diversions to large bustling amusement parks with dozens of rides. The essential ingredient in each park, though, was a carousel.

ABOVE LEFT: The 1915 Philadelphia Toboggan Company carousel at Sea Breeze Park. Unfortunately for all of us, this jewel of a carousel burned to the ground in April 1994.

BELOW LEFT: The trolley dropping off passengers at the entrance to Sea Breeze Park in Rochester, New York. Photo: courtesy of Merrick Price/Sea Breeze Park.

RIGHT: Surf Avenue near Coney Island in 1905. Photo: courtesy of Adolph Wittemann, Museum of the City of New York, The Leonard Hassam Bogart Collection.

BELOW: Henry Auchy, co-founder of the Philadelphia Toboggan Company, stands at the far right as this just-completed machine is set up at its new home in West Haven, Connecticut, in 1910. Photo: courtesy of Thomas Rebbie/PTC, Inc.

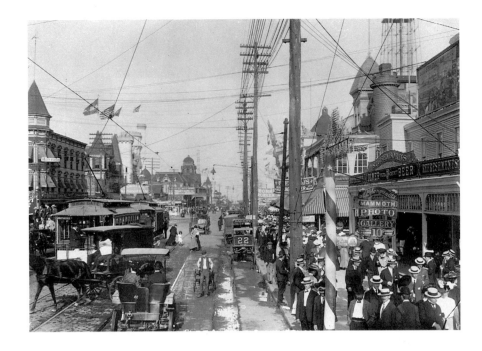

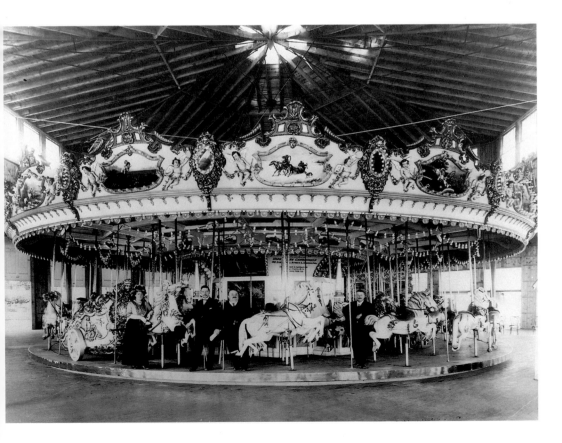

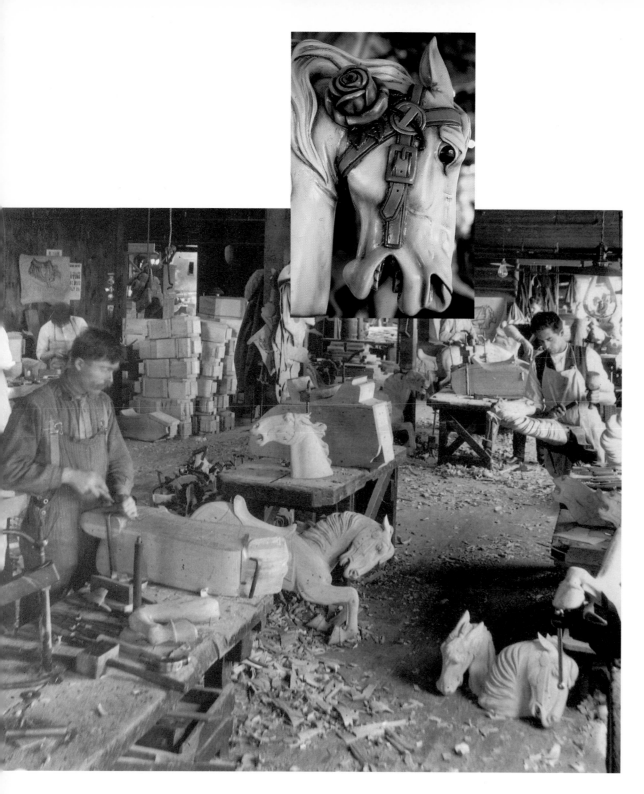

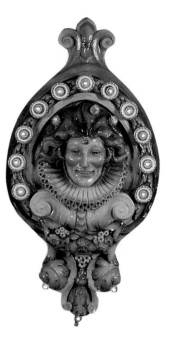

TOP LEFT: Although the Herschell-Spillman Company was best known for turning out rather simple traveling rides, its carvers were not deterred from creating beautiful horses. This rose jumper still entertains riders on the Tilden Park Carousel in Berkeley, California.

LEFT: The workshop of the Herschell-Spillman Company had an ongoing hum of activity. Each carver specialized in one aspect of the final horse; some craftsmen carved the heads while others worked on the bodies or legs. In the back left of this shop scene is a stack of horse midsections awaiting the carver's chisel. Photo: courtesy of Herschell Carousel Factory Museum.

BELOW: This smiling jester's head was a standard on the cornices of most Dentzel carousels between 1912 and 1928. The original was carved in the Dentzel factory and the subsequent shields were cast in plaster for use on dozens of carousels. Collection of Bill Finkenstein.

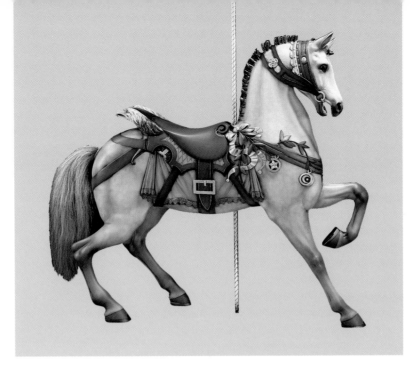

ABOVE: Grace, elegance, and realism are reflected in the work produced by the Dentzel Company, such as this outside-row stander, c. 1904. Collection of Hugh and Linda Jordan.

RIGHT: In the early days of carousel manufacturing, Gustav Dentzel and Charles Looff were both master carvers and businessmen, but as their companies grew and their time was taken up by administrative responsibilities, they hired other carvers to design and create new figures. The design of this Looff horse was most likely approved by Charles Looff, but the actual production of the figure was handled by master carver John Zalar, who worked on and off for Looff from 1904 to 1917. Freels Foundation Collection.

With this increased demand two major shifts happened in the carousel industry. First, several of the more ambitious carvers who worked for the larger companies decided to try their hand in the role of entrepreneur by starting their own companies. And second, with increased competition there was a drive to create fancier and more spectacular carousels while attempting to keep prices low.

During the early part of this new century, the well-established companies thrived. Dentzel, Looff, and the Herschell-Spillman Company (formerly the Armitage-Herschell Company) had long lists of clients and were known throughout the country for their fine work. As their reputations grew, so did the complexity of the carvings produced in their shops. Different types of animals were attempted; some were kept in the line while others were dropped. Dentzel's company produced figures of such realism that many of the figures seemed to be molded directly from the animal itself. Looff's animals became more fanciful than ever, with an array of items added to the cantle, just behind the saddle, while the Herschell-Spillman Company offered every type of carousel a park or fair owner could want, from the simplest of traveling rides to grand, ornate permanent-location machines.

Orders poured in, and only when unforeseen circumstances occurred did production become disrupted. One such problem cropped up when Gustav Dentzel died suddenly in 1909, leaving the company in a state of confusion. It took his eldest son, William, several years to straighten everything out before production started again. It was at times like this that new competitors took advantage of the misfortunes of others and began their own companies.

RIGHT: Two of the carousel's attendants posing with the Looff carousel set up at the 1915 Panama Pacific Exposition in San Francisco. Photo: courtesy of Willie Looff Taucher.

BELOW: The Philadelphia Toboggan Company rivaled Dentzel in the creation of a menagerie of realistic animals, although they only produced horses after 1908. This Saint Bernard was carved in 1906 and is one of only four dogs that came out of the company's factory. Freels Foundation Collection.

Of all the menagerie figures produced by the Dentzel Company, the cat, c. 1907, and the rabbit, c. 1910, are among the most popular with both riders and collectors. Cat: Collection of Tom and Gilda Fisher. Rabbit: Freels Foundation Collection.

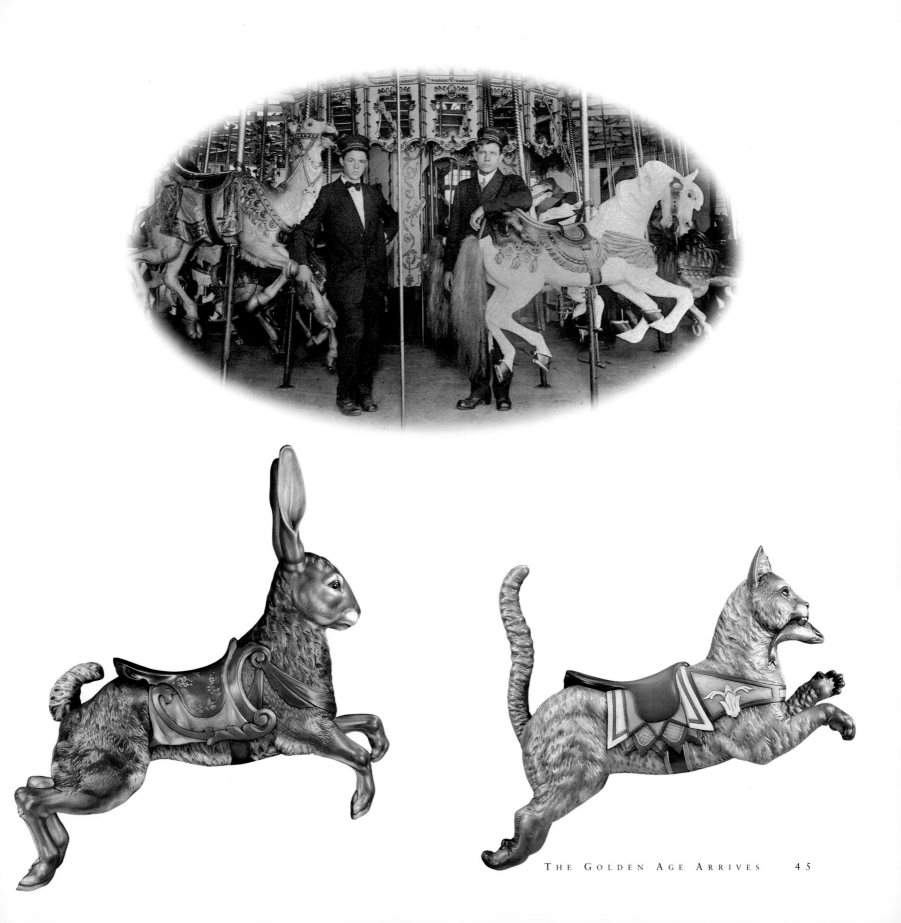

THE HERSCHELL-SPILLMAN COMPANY MENAGERIE

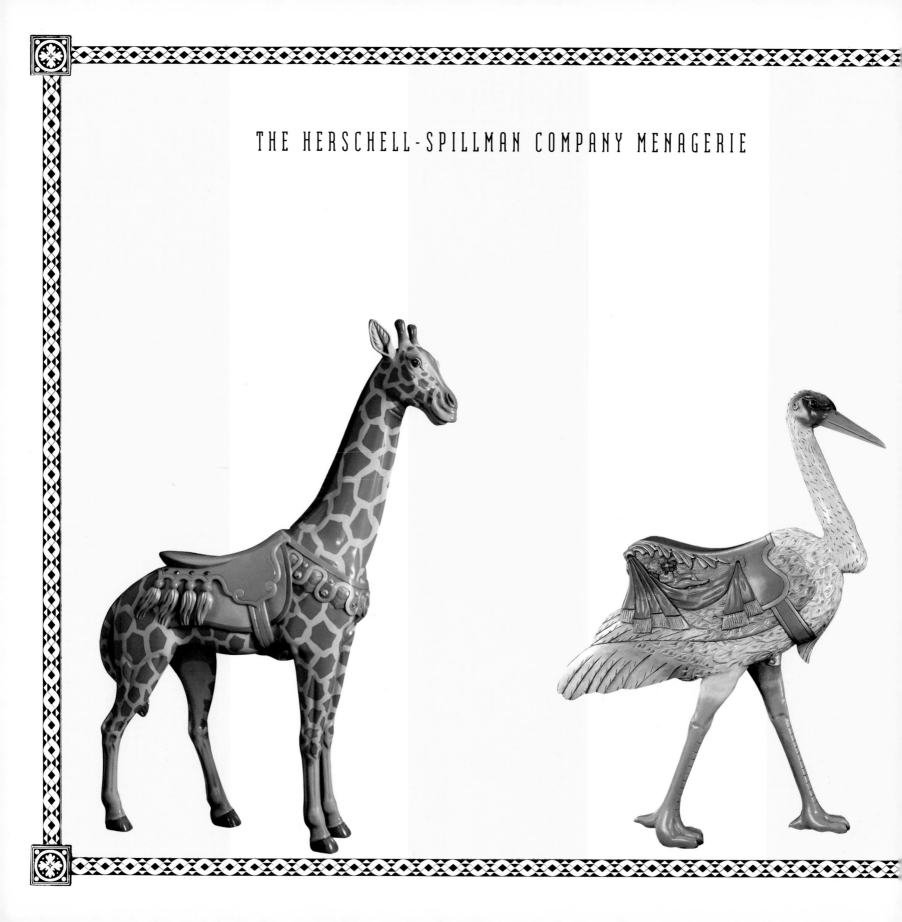

The horse was the quintessential carousel animal, not only because it was the original figure of the early French tournament practice machines, but also because it was the most familiar to ride. About 80 percent of all carousel figures made in this country were horses, but 20 percent were not. Every carousel manufacturer produced at least a few menagerie figures, but the Herschell-Spillman Company of North Tonawanda, New York, stood out by placing amazing arrays of animals on single carousels. In 1904 they switched from creating only horses to experimenting with a few different types of animals. The first were zebras, possibly because it was fairly simple to convert the mane of a horse to that of a zebra. Over the next five years other animals began to appear as options on Herschell-Spillman machines until a variety of sixteen animals could be found on some carousels.

The menagerie of both barnyard animals and more exotic creatures that can be found riding around on several Herschell-Spillman carousels includes dogs, cats, zebras, an ostrich, horses, a deer, a stork, a sea monster, pigs, giraffes, chickens, a lion, a tiger, frogs, a goat, and on rare occasions, kangaroos.

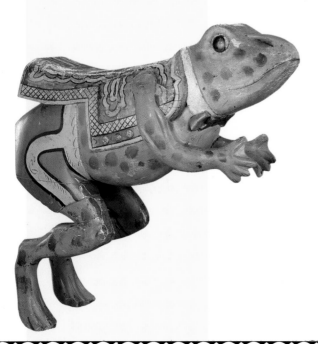

FAR RIGHT: The Illions factory paint room, filled with both completed figures and those in white primer, ready to paint. Photo: courtesy of Bernard & Bette Illions.

BACKGROUND: The M. C. Illions and Sons logo, used from 1910 until the closing of the Illions shop in 1927. Photo: courtesy of Bernard & Bette Illions.

BELOW LEFT: An Illions horse with a flying mane, similar to those found aboard the carousel at Chafatino's restaurant at Coney Island, New York. Collection of John and Cathy Daniel.

BELOW RIGHT: Marcus Charles Illions carved flamboyant horses with flying manes and flashing hooves, but the actual carving wasn't quite enough—to emphasize the unique manes he always added gold leaf. Collection of John and Cathy Daniel.

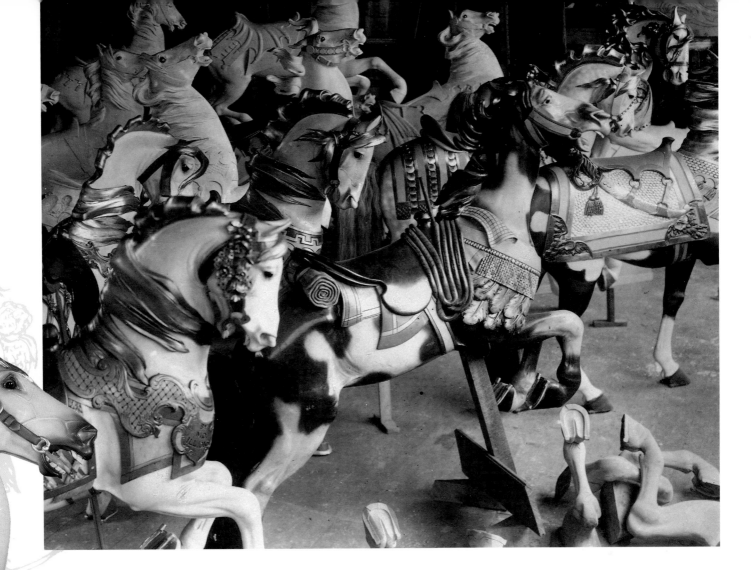

Of the new entrepreneurs, Marcus Charles Illions was the first to venture out, leaving Charles Looff's company when he was hired as a subcontractor by amusement ride innovator William Mangels. In 1900, Mangels approached Illions to undertake the tremendous job of restoring the fire-damaged Looff carousel at Feltman's of Coney Island. Illions realized he had a chance to show the world his formidable abilities as a master craftsman. The result was the most spectacular carousel that had been built to date. The replacement horses struck dramatic, animated poses and featured jewel-laden trappings expertly carved in relief, expressive faces, and thick, cascading manes. This ornate interpretation was to characterize Illions's style throughout his career.

After a dispute with the city of New York in 1905, Charles Looff moved his factory to Riverside, Rhode Island. One of the carvers that he left behind was Charles Carmel, who decided to follow the lead of Illions and open his own shop. Carmel picked an area near the stables in Brooklyn's Prospect Park so that he was never far from good models. As with many of the smaller shops, Carmel was not set up to produce the complicated mechanical aspects of a carousel, so most of his work was done for other businesses, which made the frames and mechanisms, bought the animals from Carmel, and put their name on the finished carousels. This practice led to a number of what are called mixed machines, such as the carousels put together by Thomas Murphy, M. D. Borrelli, and Fred Dolle. Most of Murphy's carousels had at least some Carmel-style horses.

Carmel's career bounced back and forth between filling special orders for the frame companies and working for other manufacturers such as Illions and Stein and Goldstein. His name also appeared on the payrolls of D. C. Müller and the Philadelphia Toboggan Company.

Carmel's one attempt at having his own carousel ended in disaster. After saving enough to build his own machine, he created an exquisite carousel, which he placed in Coney Island's Dreamland Park. The evening before the 1911 season was to open, the entire park burned to the ground, including Carmel's beautiful and uninsured carousel.

Solomon Stein and Harry Goldstein, both Russian immigrants and accomplished woodworkers, met in 1905 when they were employed by William Mangels at his Carousel Works. After developing their carousel-carving skills for a few years, the two struck out on their own and formed a partnership in 1907, eventually leading to the formation of the Artistic Caroussel Manufacturing Company.

Stein and Goldstein were certainly influenced by their Coney Island contemporaries, namely Looff and Illions. However, the two soon developed a unique style of carving—big! Stein and Goldstein only carved horses: massive, fierce steeds that strained at the bit. But in stark contrast to the aggressive look of the animals, the bridles and trappings often featured delicately carved flowers in deep relief, feathers, tassels, and oversized buckles.

The partners eventually constructed seventeen carousels, eleven of which they owned and operated. Like their horses, many of Stein and Goldstein's carousels were also big, often carrying five rows of horses and seating as many as eighty people.

TOP LEFT AND RIGHT: Although Charles Carmel carved for many different companies in a variety of styles, he worked in his own distinctive style when he had a free reign in design. The two shown here are from the carousel at Playland in Rye, New York, a good example of some of Carmel's finest designs and carvings.

BOTTOM LEFT: Large buckles, deep relief flowers, and almond-shaped eyes were the distinctive trademarks of the horses carved by Solomon Stein and Harry Goldstein, but design and craftsmanship were only two of the talents of this partnership, which also set up and operated amusement rides all along the East Coast. Collection of Charlotte Dinger.

BOTTOM RIGHT: Occasionally a carousel company would create a sample horse to take to trade shows or to display in its offices. This flowered stander from the Artistic Caroussel Manufacturing Company is just such a figure, not only displaying the carving talents of Stein and Goldstein, but also showing their address.

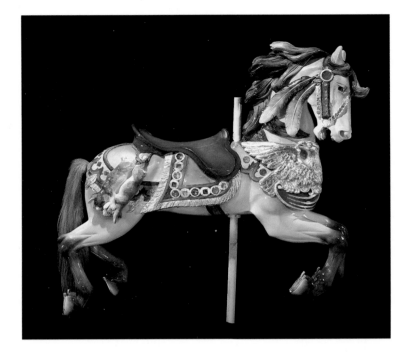

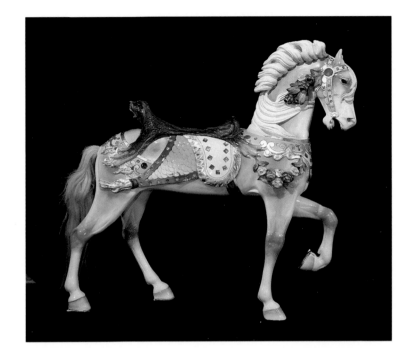

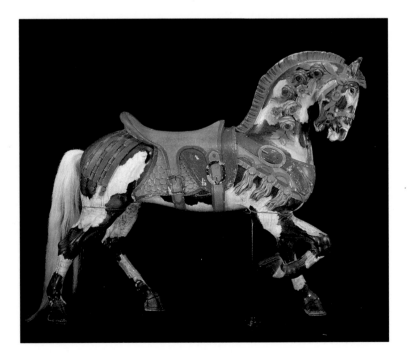

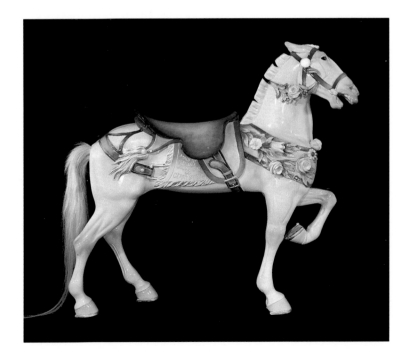

While the carousel industry was flourishing in Brooklyn, Philadelphia was also expanding with two new companies. In 1900 liquor distributor Henry Auchy was looking to diversify his business, and the burgeoning amusement industry appeared to be the way to go. He and a business partner, Chester Albright, bought what wooden animals remained in the stock of the short-lived E. Joy Morris Carousel Company. They then hired former Dentzel employees Daniel and Alfred Müller as their main carvers. Perhaps because of Auchy's business savvy, his new business, the Philadelphia Toboggan Company, was one of only two companies to survive the various economic turmoils of the next thirty years and is still in business.

For two years the Müller brothers created carousel figures exclusively for Auchy before deciding to start their own company, D. C. Müller and Bro. Even though a portion of the Müllers' business was the continued carving of figures for the Philadelphia Toboggan Company, there were now three official companies, including the Dentzel Company, manufacturing carousels in the Philadelphia area.

As the carousel makers of Coney Island and Philadelphia were creating wonderfully fancy carousels that would be installed in amusement parks throughout the country, two other companies were kept very busy turning out smaller traveling machines. Between the Herschell-Spillman Company and the C. W. Parker Amusement Company, about one new carousel per week was finding its way into fairs, carnivals, and circuses. These rides ranged anywhere from eighteen smaller horses on a simple platform to fifty-four figures, sometimes including a wide variety of animals, revolving on a light-filled machine.

By 1910, both the country's economy and the amusement business were booming, and carousel production was more than keeping pace. Hundreds of new parks and fairs opened each year. If one of the carousel companies experienced a slow down, they would just continue to create figures, knowing full well that a new customer could appear at any time. Even several years later, as the specter of war crept across Europe, carousels continued to be shipped on a regular basis.

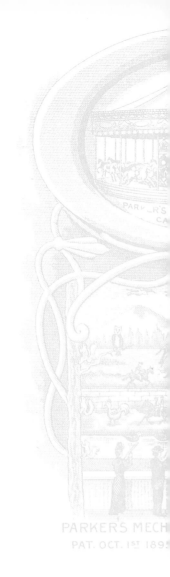

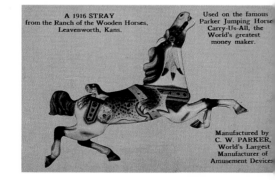

A 1916 STRAY
from the Ranch of the Wooden Horses,
Leavenworth, Kans.

Used on the famous Parker Jumping Horse Carry-Us-All, the World's greatest money maker.

Manufactured by
C. W. PARKER,
World's Largest
Manufacturer of
Amusement Devices

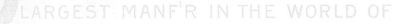

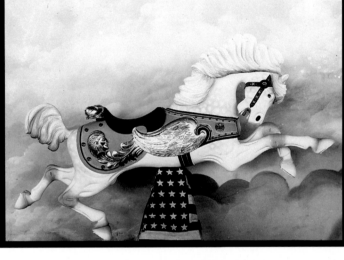

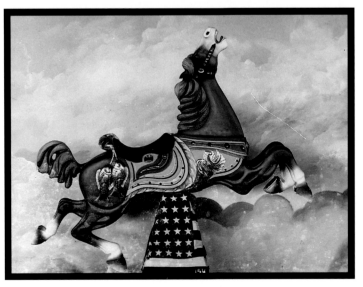

BACKGROUND: Letterhead from C. W. Parker.

LEFT: C. W. Parker produced a variety of postcards for promoting his carousels.

RIGHT: Factory photographs from the C. W. Parker Amusement Company, c. 1914. Photos: courtesy of Staples & Charles.

C. W. PARKER

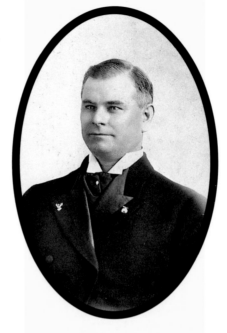

Charles Parker, or "Colonel Parker," as he liked to be called, was a dynamic entrepreneur who enjoyed the showman side of his work. He must have admired P. T. Barnum since he fashioned his business practices after the great promoter.

Every trick was used to convince the customer of the greatness of both the C. W. Parker Amusement Company and of the man himself. Production was exaggerated, buildings were shown to be larger than actual size, profits made by his rides were purported to be enormous, and the figure of the man himself was always portrayed as gargantuan. He used an image of his house on a souvenir postcard since, no doubt, everyone would want a photograph of this historic home. And every aspect of his business life was photographically documented because of its momentous importance.

One promotional poster shows Parker standing over a vast manufacturing empire complete with multiple smokestacks and four fully loaded trains filled with Parker rides. The accompanying caption reads, "The Amusement King, C. W. Parker, & His Mammoth Factories."

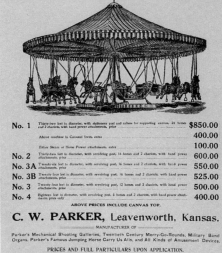

PARKER'S Flying Horse Swing

No. 1	Thirty-two feet in diameter, with stationary post and rafters for supporting canvas, 24 horses and 2 chariots, with hand power attachments, price	$850.00
	Above machine in Carousel form, extra	400.00
	Either Steam or Horse Power attachments, extra	100.00
No. 2	Thirty-two feet in diameter, with revolving post, 16 horses and 2 chariots, with hand power attachments, price	600.00
No. 3A	Twenty-six feet in diameter, with revolving post, 16 horses and 2 chariots, with hand power attachments, price	550.00
No. 3B	Twenty-four feet in diameter, with revolving post, 16 horses and 2 chariots, with hand power attachments, price	525.00
No. 3	Twenty-four feet in diameter, with revolving post, 12 horses and 3 chariots, with hand power attachments, price	500.00
No. 4	Eighteen feet in diameter, with revolving post, 8 horses and 2 chariots, with hand power attachments, price only	400.00

ABOVE PRICES INCLUDE CANVAS TOP.

C. W. PARKER, Leavenworth, Kansas.

MANUFACTURER OF

Parker's Mechanical Shooting Galleries, Twentieth Century Merry-Go-Rounds, Military Band Organs, Parker's Famous Jumping Horse Carry Us Alls, and All Kinds of Amusement Devices.

PRICES AND FULL PARTICULARS UPON APPLICATION.

LEFT: A PORTRAIT OF A YOUNG CHARLES W. PARKER AT THE TIME THAT HE WAS PUTTING TOGETHER HIS AMUSEMENT "EMPIRE." PHOTO: COURTESY OF STAPLES & CHARLES.

ABOVE: THIS MIDSIZED FLOWERED PARKER IS TYPICAL OF THE STRETCHED-OUT GAIT AND WILD LOOK OF MOST OF PARKER'S HORSES. COLLECTION OF WALTER AND MARY LAWRENCE YOUREE.

RIGHT: ADVERTISING AND SELF-PROMOTION WERE TWO OF PARKER'S STRONG POINTS. THIS IS A HANDOUT PRODUCED TO HELP SELL ONE OF HIS SMALLER CAROUSELS. COURTESY OF THE SUMMIT COLLECTION.

It wasn't until the United States went to the aid of its allies that the orders for new machines began to wane. Not only did the orders slow down, but the endless supplies of good lumber that the carvers had come to count on were going for more immediate uses, such as gun stocks, airplane propellers, soldiers' barracks, and anything else which could help win the Great War. The crowds of people who had been frequenting the parks also turned their attention away from being amused to face the serious tasks of war. Some of the carousel companies did their bit by converting areas of their manufacturing operations to the creation of items needed for the war effort, but their equipment was, for the most part, ill-suited for the kind of production needed by the military.

The war was followed by a brief but deep recession, which slowed the amusement industry's recovery even further. During this time the Müllers closed shop and went back to work for William Dentzel; Charles Looff died and the family closed the manufacturing side of the company to concentrate on the operation of their amusement parks; and Parker's "empire" began to falter, feeling the effects of too much bravado and too little business savvy.

By 1922 the Dentzel and Philadelphia Toboggan Company shops were back in full swing. The Herschell-Spillman Company had split into two successful entities, the Allan Herschell Company and the Spillman Engineering Corporation, each turning out well-crafted traveling carousels. But despite this apparent resurgence, the era of the carousel maker had quietly slipped by. Orders were not pouring into the factories, and the people who were out to buy were looking for bargains. Creativity was giving way to mass production. Assembly-line Model A's were chugging down streets and Kodak Brownies were found in the hands of many tourists. The sense of artistic drama in the production of a carousel was replaced, for the most part, by the ideas of fast production and quick profits.

The general public had also turned its attention to the era of flappers, the Charleston, and bathtub gin. This new and risqué way of life made the now tame entertainment of whirling on a carousel pale in comparison. The times were changing and so was the carousel. The thrill of this once exotic machine was being replaced with a sense of romance. The carousel had become a ride for children and for lovers, for young and old, and for anyone who cared to dream. The golden age of the carousel maker had passed, but the love of carousels would only continue to grow.

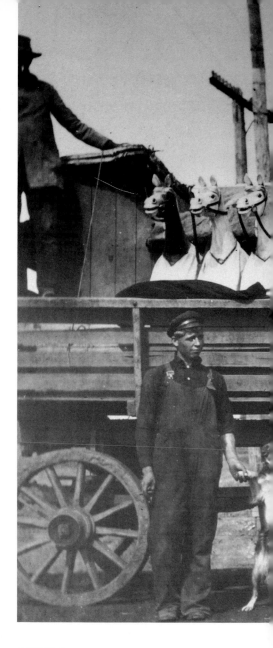

ABOVE: A TRAVELING CAROUSEL MEANT EXACTLY THAT. MOST CAROUSELS WENT FROM TOWN TO TOWN BY RAILROAD. BUT THIS EARLY HERSCHELL-SPILLMAN MACHINE WAS TRANSPORTED BY HORSE AND CART. PHOTO: COURTESY OF JOHN AND JAN DAVIS.

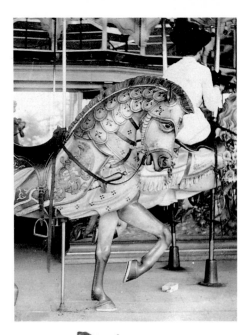

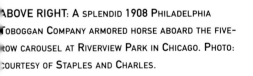

ABOVE RIGHT: A SPLENDID 1908 PHILADELPHIA TOBOGGAN COMPANY ARMORED HORSE ABOARD THE FIVE-ROW CAROUSEL AT RIVERVIEW PARK IN CHICAGO. PHOTO: COURTESY OF STAPLES AND CHARLES.

RIGHT: PATRIOTIC THEMES WERE USED TO DECORATE A VARIETY OF FIGURES, BUT RARELY WERE THE CARVINGS AS BOLD AND DYNAMIC AS THE EAGLE WRAPPED AROUND THE FRONT OF THIS PHILADELPHIA TOBOGGAN COMPANY STANDING HORSE, CREATED BY FRANK CARRETTA, C. 1915. FREELS FOUNDATION COLLECTION.

A DAY AT THE FACTORY

❊❊❊❊❊❊❊❊❊❊❊❊❊❊❊❊❊❊

CHAPTER 4

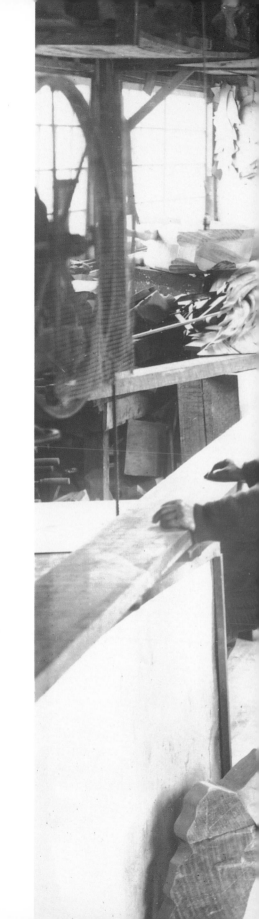

Author's note: In 1899 a writer for the New York Times Sunday Magazine *visited a carousel factory in Brooklyn. The subsequent article was brief and rather vague about the inner workings of an actual carousel company, but that article started me wondering what a work day might have been like. Drawn from a series of interviews with relatives of craftsmen and people who had actually been to one or more of the factories, and hundreds of pieces of information and photographs from a variety of sources, this chapter is an attempt to pay a visit to a carousel factory.*

THE WORKSHOP OF M.C. ILLIONS. C. 1922. PHOTO: COURTESY OF BERNARD AND BETTE ILLIONS.

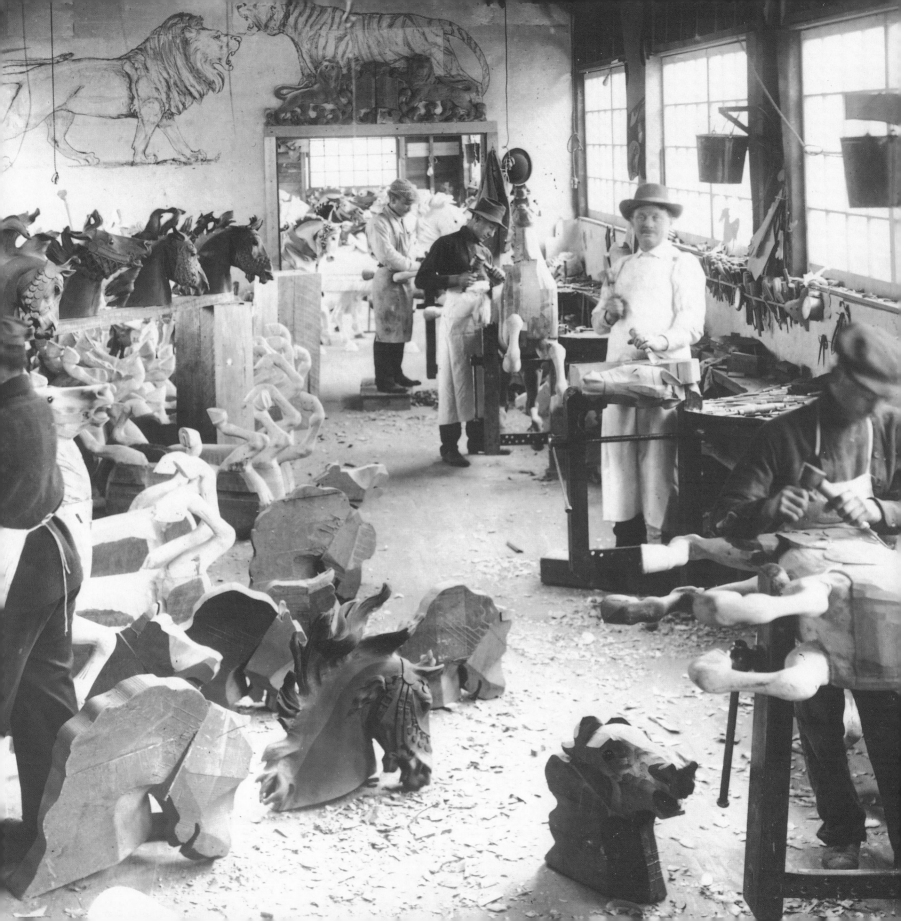

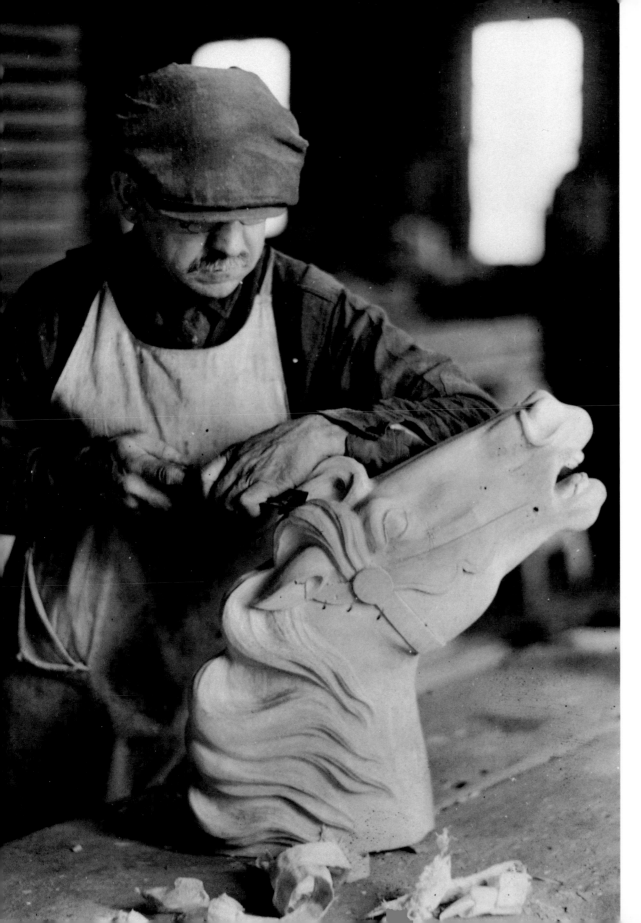

C. F. KOPP FINISHING A HEAD FOR A SPILLMAN
ENGINEERING CAROUSEL HORSE, C. 1920. PHOTO: COURTESY
OF SMITHSONIAN INSTITUTION

The winter of 1905 has been harsher than usual, and although it is officially spring, the last days of March are not any warmer than the first days. The Northeast has been blanketed in snow for six weeks straight, and each day the icy road to work seems to stretch out further and further.

The craftsmen arrive at the factory as the first light begins to seep through the cloud cover. Sometimes in small groups, but mostly as solitary figures, they come through the doors. After shedding their coats and hats, they head straight for the pot of coffee, not so much to drink but to warm their hands with hot cups. Gathered around the single cast-iron stove filled with glowing embers, they begin to warm up. So does the conversation—politics, the weather, health, and who thinks who drank too much last Sunday. This sets the stage for conversations that last the entire day as points and counterpoints are exchanged between workbenches and from carving room to paint room.

Since the opening day for amusement parks fast approaches and the deadline for shipping the new carousels is looming, the work day will be another long one, probably twelve hours. The men will stop only now and then for a brief rest, for something to eat, or perhaps just long enough to make a point about one of the day's topics. Except for a few new workers who have been called in to help complete the current projects, everyone knows what he has to do.

With morning greetings over, the men of the carousel cinch their apron ties and head off to a day's work. They approach their stations, passing partially carved wooden animals that lie scattered in pieces about the workshop. Although the rooms are brightly lit by bare light bulbs dangling from the ceiling, everyone is delighted as the sun breaks through the clouds and sends a shower of welcome warmth and light through the cold morning air.

Drawings of full-sized carousel animals in various poses hang on the walls like a vast two-dimensional zoo. In between these sketches are signs describing new power tools, calendars with deadlines marked in red, and odd scraps of lumber. Several metal buckets filled with the fine sand used for putting out small fires dangle overhead. The boards of the hardwood floor have been swept clean from the previous day's work but will soon be covered with hundreds of flying chips.

In one corner, a craftsman begins preparations for cutting out the basic shapes of the animals' heads, bodies, and legs. He selects the best wood from the large stack of basswood stored against the wall, checking each length for knots or

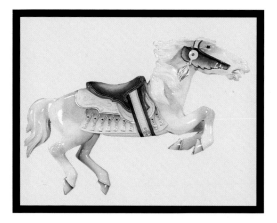

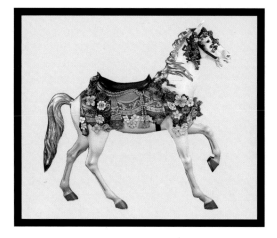

TOP: An outside-row Allan Herschell Company horse, c. 1921, recently restored by R & F Design of Bristol, Connecticut.

BOTTOM: This flower covered horse, c. 1924, is one of three carved by M. C. Illions for use on his "Supreme Machines." It is now in the collection of John and Cathy Daniel.

irregularities in the grain. Then, after carefully tracing the outline of the leg or head, he skillfully guides the wood through the rasping teeth of a huge band saw. Once the wood has been cut, the pieces are passed along to the area were they will be glued together.

Earlier this morning, an apprentice prepared the glue by placing a two-gallon pot over a gas burner and then slowly adding chunks of a hard, caramel-colored substance. As the solid glue began to heat, it turned to a liquid with the consistency of molasses. The craftsman in charge of glue-up fills a small container from that now hot pot. He then covers the surfaces of the freshly cut wood with a thin coat of the hot glue. Quickly clamping the wood together, he applies just the right amount of pressure so that a line of glue presses out of the seam where the pieces meet. Within minutes a glued silhouette of a horse's head, wrapped in clamps, is on a rack to cool and dry.

Nearby, a neatly stacked pile of heads is waiting for the carver. The master carver soon tells an apprentice to bring one over, then secures it to the workbench by the jaws of a large vise. Studying the prototype of the head he will copy, the carver quickly begins to chip away large chunks of wood and within fifteen minutes the rough features of the face start to emerge. Working at a steady pace, the carver knows precisely how hard to pound the back of his gouge. Once the basic shape is completed, he makes a selection from the dozens of tools on his bench and proceeds to carve the detail that will determine the character of the horse he is creating. The flow of the mane, the look of the eye, and the shape of the mouth are all critical to the final product. By noon, the head is finished and it is time for lunch.

The noontime air is filled with the sounds of the great American melting pot. Conversations in Italian, German, and Yiddish mix with bits of heavily accented

The Herschell-Spillman Company carving room, c. 1914. Photo: courtesy of Herschell Carousel Factory Museum.

A jumping horse designed and carved by Daniel Müller, with its original paint. Corey Collection.

English. Peppered salamis, fresh dumplings, and pickled herring are pulled from the canvas lunch bags, leading to barters and trades of various food. Soon all the men are satisfied with the meals they have put together, and the serious business of eating begins.

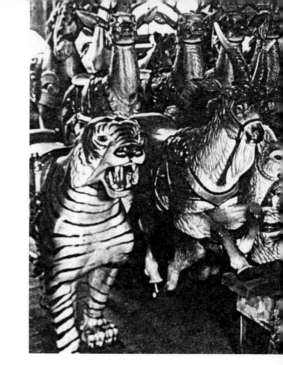

Their appetites satisfied, the men return to work. The finished wooden head is sent back to glue-up along with a newly carved body and four completed legs. Wooden pegs (dowels) are added to the head and legs while holes are drilled in the surface of the body where these recently carved pieces will be placed. The contact areas are then covered with the hot hide glue, and the segments of the horse are clamped together and set aside to dry.

It is then the finishing carver's job to complete the area around the glue joints. This is not always easy, especially on animals covered with fur, such as a rabbit, cat, or goat. Since each carver has his own distinct style, trying to match the fur of the leg and head to that of the body can be very difficult. Most of the time the finish carver attempts to make a transition from one style to the other.

With quick sanding, what only yesterday had been thirty individual pieces of wood has been transformed into a wild galloping steed with a flying mane and flashing hooves. It has taken a total of thirty-five hours put in by a half dozen expert craftsmen to create this figure, which will now journey into an adjacent room where the painting process awaits.

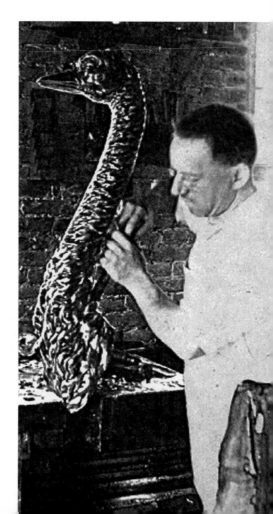

Once in the paint room the horse receives several coats of white lead paint. Any imperfections that might remain in the wood's surface are filled in with these base coats. After another sanding with a fine-grain sandpaper, the painter has a smooth, porous surface on which to work. He then creates colors by mixing various "Japan" color pigments with varnish, a drying agent, and more of the lead-base paint.

Selecting a horse that is primed and ready to paint, the artist applies the body colors first. Dapple gray is by far the most popular color but is also the most time-consuming. The process involves dipping one half of a wide brush into one color and the other half into a different color. The painter then stipples with the brush by dabbing or poncing in a tight circle, putting the lighter colored paint to the inside of the circle. This gives a dappled effect by making an undefined line between the light and dark colors, much like the hair on a real horse. When the body colors are completed, the painter steps back to admire his horse. His work

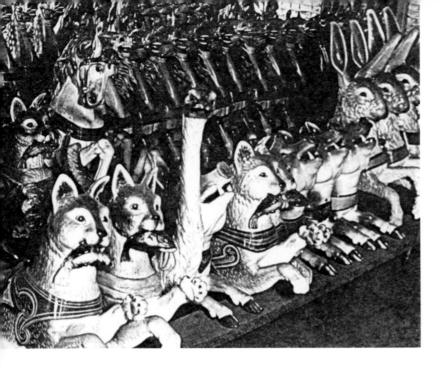

has been so precise and his methods so exacting that there is hardly any paint on his hands or the apron covering his still-fresh white shirt, tie, or neatly pressed pants.

If gold or silver leaf is to be used the painter applies it now, after the body color is finished and before the trappings are colored. This way he can coat the leaf with a wash of color if it is called for. He first places sizing, a glue-like substance, on the area where leaf will be placed, allowing it to dry for several hours before cautiously applying the leaf. Once it has been gently laid onto the sizing, the painter burnishes the leaf with a soft brush for a sparkle and shine that cannot be matched.

ABOVE: A FULL CAROUSEL'S WORTH OF DENTZEL ANIMALS WAITING TO BE SHIPPED OUT. C. 1922. PHOTO: COURTESY OF MR. AND MRS. WILLIAM DENTZEL AND FAMILY.

RIGHT: WORKING NEAR THE NATURAL LIGHT PROVIDED BY AN OPEN WINDOW, MÜLLER FINISHES THE DETAILS OF A MANE ON ONE OF HIS HORSE'S HEADS. PHOTO: COURTESY OF MR. AND MRS. WILLIAM DENTZEL AND FAMILY.

LEFT: SALVATORE CERNIGLIARO AT THE DENTZEL COMPANY, WORKING ON THE FEATHERS OF AN OSTRICH NECK. C. 1922. PHOTO: COURTESY OF MR. AND MRS. WILLIAM DENTZEL AND FAMILY.

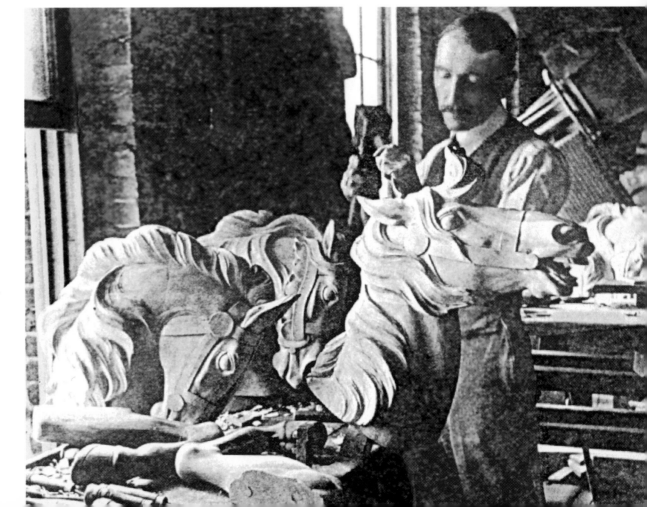

The painter's next challenge is to apply color to the trappings. He reaches for a large, worn leather book kept nearby that is filled with colored sketches of different bits and pieces of carousel animal trappings. He selects a color scheme that not only works with the dapples of this particular horse, but fits well with the color design he has devised for the entire carousel. Once the colors are chosen the painter works quickly, holding several brushes in one hand while applying the appropriate color with the other. Before the afternoon is over, the colors are complete. Over the next few days the horse will receive two coats of clear spar varnish before being shipped off to its first ride on the carousel itself.

Meanwhile, the workers at the loading bay are deftly packing the final pieces of a full machine finished only last week. The animals are carefully packed four to a crate and then placed in freight cars just outside the dock. The metal gears, cranks, and motor have already been shipped to the amusement park by the machine shop across town. Only a few hours are left to load the remainder of the carousel since the freight cars are scheduled to be picked up by 8:00 P.M. The sixteen wedge-shaped sections of the carousel platform have been stacked nearby. With one man at each corner, the sections are moved into the train and set on edge before being secured to the car's side. The crew finishes just as the locomotive backs up to the lead car. The doors are closed, and the train heads off into the night.

It is dark now. The master carver carefully inspects each one of the precious tools that he brought with him on his trek across the Atlantic. Any nick or dullness is noted to an apprentice. The tools will be sharpened and honed to perfect working order by morning. The artist's paintbrushes are thoroughly cleaned and set upright to dry to preserve the bristles. A shovel full of coal is placed in the stove so that the freshly painted figures will continue to dry overnight.

Heavy winter overcoats take the place of shop aprons, and thick woolen scarves are wrapped snugly around necks. Goodnights and well-wishes pass around as the last few points of the day's topics are made. The carvers, painters, carpenters, and general woodworkers file out the same doors that they entered over twelve hours before and head toward home. As they make their way through the crystal clear, crisp night air, unknowingly they leave behind a portion of a legacy that will add happiness to thousands of lives and that will eventually become part of a heritage cherished for decades to come.

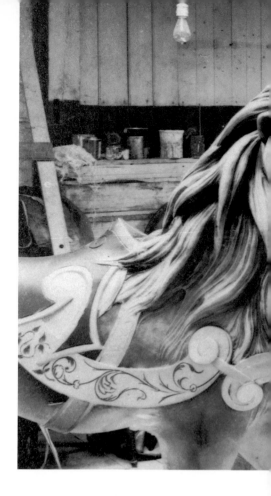

ABOVE: The paint room of the Philadelphia Toboggan Company, c. 1905. Photo: courtesy of Thomas Rebbie/PTC, Inc.

RIGHT: Applying the white, lead-based primer at the Allan Herschell Company, c. 1919. Photo: courtesy of Smithsonian Institution.

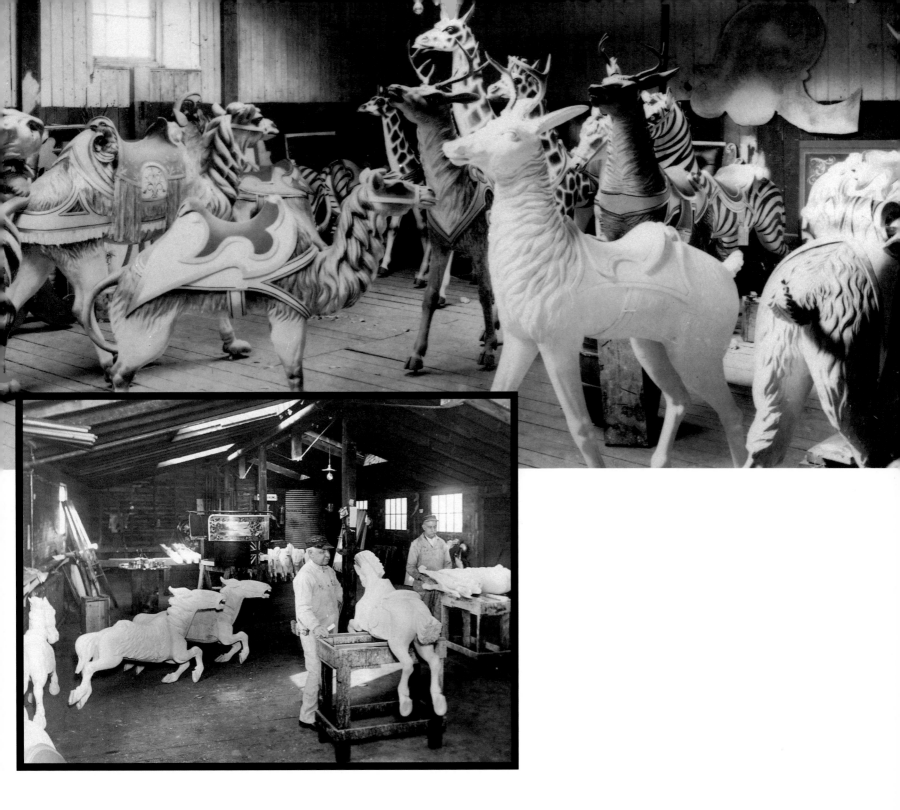

THE MASTER CARVERS

❋❋❋❋❋❋❋❋❋❋❋❋❋❋❋

CHAPTER 5

Every carousel company filled its wood shop

with highly skilled craftsmen—men who spent most of their

lives with a chisel in their hands, shaving chips of wood

from large square blocks, out of which would come amaz-

ing animals, cherubs, mythological beasts, detailed cavalry

saddles, and a vast array of other wonderful creations.

During their years of training they would learn the intimate

aspects of wood, the flow of the grain, and how each type

of hardwood reacts to the tools that became extensions of

their hands. And in those hands, a sharpened gouge could

flow through wood like a table knife through soft butter.

ALTHOUGH IT IS NOT KNOWN HOW SOME OF THE LESSER-KNOWN CARVERS INFLUENCED THE STYLES OF THE MAJOR CARVING SHOPS, THE EFFECTS OF THEIR TALENTS MUST HAVE BEEN SIGNIFICANT. HERE, MASTER CARVER CHARLES LEOPOLD, WHO CARVED FOR BOTH DENTZEL AND MÜLLER, PUTS THE FINISHING TOUCH ON A HORSE IN THE MÜLLER SHOP. PHOTO: COURTESY OF SMITHSONIAN INSTITUTION.

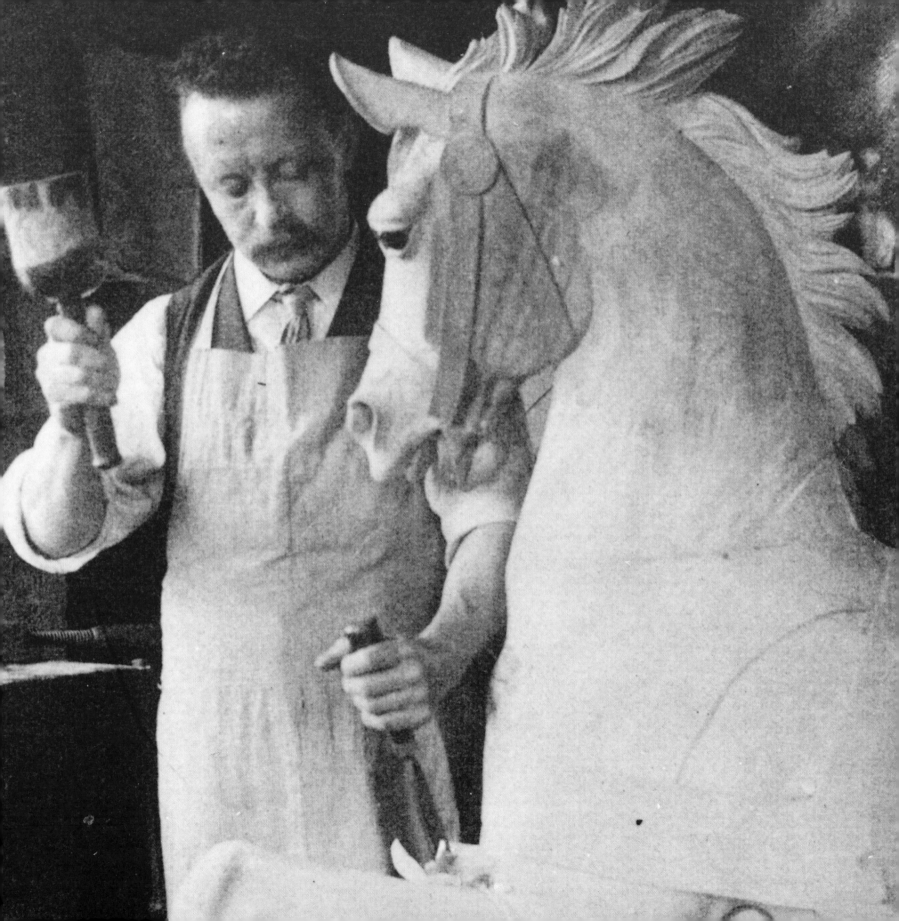

In a matter of hours they could copy almost any prototype in exacting detail so that it was impossible to tell which was the original and which was the copy.

Out of this group of very talented people came a number of extraordinary craftsmen whose mastery of carving tools was matched by their artistic and design abilities. In the highly competitive world of carousel manufacturing, the capacity for design was critical for success, especially in the fancier, larger carousels produced by Dentzel, Looff, Illions, and the other high-end carousel makers. On carousels such as these it was rare to find the same design on any two outside-row figures. Since each carousel was unique in its trappings there was an almost endless number of designs. How many ways could the fairly simple equipment for a horse be re-designed, and how many different types of clowns or animals could be attached to lions' sides or behind camels' saddles? The number of variations that they devised continues to be astounding, because only a handful of these craftsmen did the actual designing.

Although the basic motivation to produce carousels may have been the need to make a living, the drive to create, for these few select craftsmen, must have gone well past the bounds of just making money. There is no doubt that the sculpting of wooden figures represented an expression of the maker as an artist. The exacting detail, the sweeping flamboyance, and the sensuous grace and beauty of many of the figures created by these men reveal an ambition beyond the creation of a seat on an amusement park ride.

Several of their names are familiar from the titles of the companies, such as M. C. Illions and Sons or D. C. Müller and Bro. Others were carousel makers who chose to stay less visible, such as Harry Goldstein and Solomon Stein of the Artistic Caroussel Manufacturing Company or Charles Carmel, who worked for a variety of other companies on a freelance basis. Some worked in the shadows of their employers, such as John Zalar, who carved both for Charles Looff and for the Philadelphia Toboggan Company; or Frank Carretta, whose designs dramatically changed the Philadelphia Toboggan Company's style of horses; and of course Salvatore Cernigliaro, who created exquisitely detailed carvings for the short-lived E. Joy Morris Carousel Company and then spent the next twenty-eight years working for Dentzel, Müller, and the Philadelphia Toboggan Company. There were Charles Leopold, first at Dentzel's and later at Müller's, Eugene Drisco at C. W. Parker, and still others whose names have been lost but whose designs have been etched into the multifaceted history of the carousel.

RIGHT: THIS OUTSIDE-ROW STANDING HORSE, C. 1906, IS AN EXAMPLE OF THE WORK CHERNY PRODUCED FOR THE DENTZEL COMPANY. OUTSTANDING FIGURES ON THE SIDES OF ANIMALS, AS SEEN HERE, HAVE BEEN NAMED "CHERNY FIGURES" IN HONOR OF THIS GREAT CARVER. FREELS FOUNDATION COLLECTION.

SALVATORE CERNIGLIARO

As a furniture carver and cabinetmaker in Palermo, Italy, Salvatore (Cherny) Cernigliaro spent his teenage years learning his craft from master craftsmen. He learned well, but his interests lay beyond the shores of Italy. At the age of twenty-three, despite knowing he suffered from acute seasickness, he ventured across the Atlantic to the golden shores of America.

Soon after his arrival he found a job working for the E. Joy Morris Carousel Company in Philadelphia where he was able to transform his furniture-carving talents into those of a carousel maker. Unfortunately, Cherny joined the company only a few months before it was sold and soon found himself out of a job.

Several months went by before he entered the gate of Gustav Dentzel's prosperous carousel company. Using the only English words he knew, Cherny asked Mr. Dentzel for a job as a carver in his factory. Cherny walked away disappointed only to find out a week later that Dentzel had offered him a job on the spot, but he had interpreted Gustav's rather gruff manner as a no.

In his work for Dentzel, Cherny brought the addition of flamboyant baroque relief carvings to many of the outside-row figures. His carvings of flowing ribbons, Rubenesque cherubs, and dancing clowns are readily identifiable and carry the endearing term "Cherny figure."

Cherny kept busy for the next sixty-five years. When orders were slow at the Dentzel Company, Cherny could be found working either for the Philadelphia Toboggan Company or for Daniel Müller. During World War I, when carousel production was very limited, he was occupied with the precision carving of hundreds of airplane propellers. After 1930, he moved to California and used his talents to train others in the art and woodcarving.

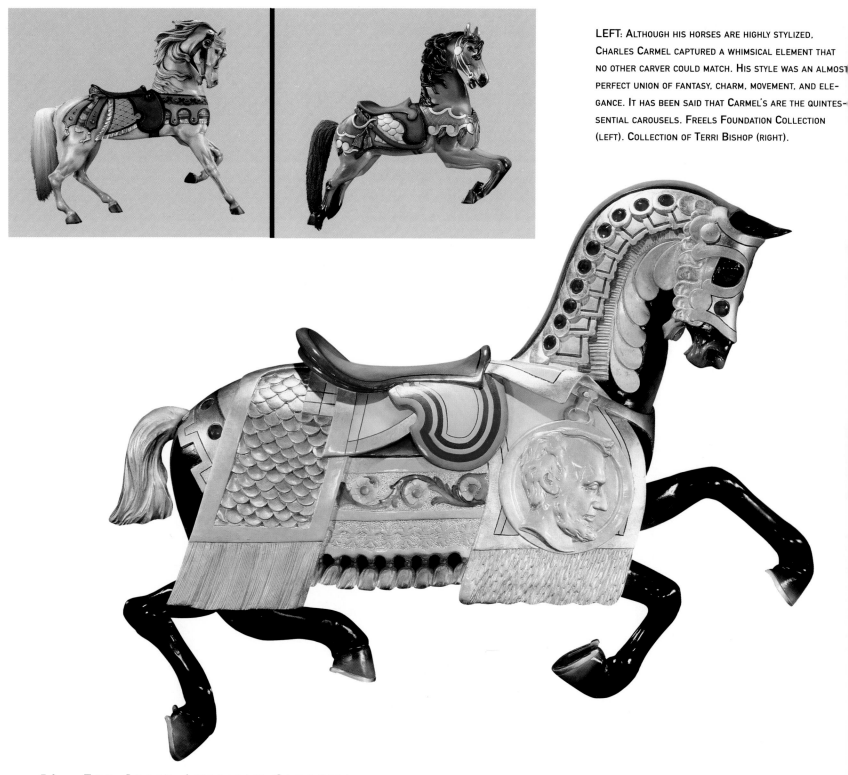

LEFT: Although his horses are highly stylized, Charles Carmel captured a whimsical element that no other carver could match. His style was an almost perfect union of fantasy, charm, movement, and elegance. It has been said that Carmel's are the quintessential carousels. Freels Foundation Collection (left). Collection of Terri Bishop (right).

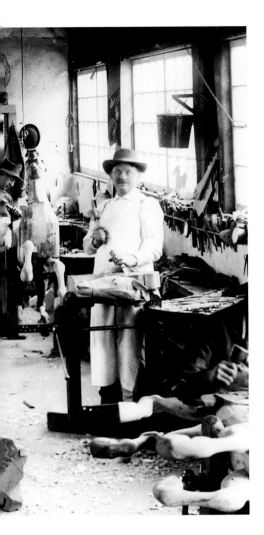

ABOVE: MARCUS CHARLES ILLIONS LOOKS UP FROM HIS WORKBENCH WHERE HE WORKS ON THE HEAD OF A HORSE. ACCORDING TO ILLIONS'S SONS, HE WAS THE ONLY ONE IN THE SHOP ALLOWED TO CARVE HORSE'S HEADS, SINCE THE PERSONALITY OF THE FIGURE WOULD ALWAYS BE FINALIZED IN THE EXPRESSION. PHOTO: COURTESY OF BERNARD AND BETTE ILLIONS.

OPPOSITE LEFT: ILLIONS CARVED FEW ARMORED HORSES, BUT WHEN HE DID THEY WERE SPECTACULAR. THE LINCOLN PORTRAIT ON THE SIDE OF THIS FIGURE MAKES IT ONE OF THE TRUE MASTERPIECES OF CAROUSEL ART. NEW ENGLAND CAROUSEL MUSEUM.

To narrow this list down any further is difficult, yet there are three names which come up time and again when discussing the artistic direction of the carousel in this country. Those are M. C. Illions, John Zalar, and Daniel Müller.

Marcus Charles Illions's talents as a craftsman and artist were legendary around the amusement industry in Coney Island. His expertise in creating carousel figures was matched by his tenacity and perfectionism. Despite an increasing demand for his machines, he insisted on carving all the heads himself and most of the bodies of the fancier outside-row figures. Although these self-imposed rules limited production, there was certainly no mistaking who was in charge and who designed the figures that came from the Illions shop. The limited number of carousels created by Illions helped to produce an impression of scarcity, making an M. C. Illions and Sons carousel the most highly prized of all the Coney Island machines. Eventually ten separate locations in Coney Island operated Illions carousels at one time during the late 1920s.

The Illions workshop was small and staffed mostly by the immediate family, although there were three or four full-time non-Illions employees. When they were old enough, Illions's four sons were given various jobs in the factory, and on the occasion of looming deadlines, a variety of relatives would be called in to assist.

Driven to perform, Illions was a caring and generous man to those who were loyal, but his tolerance for lackluster work or mistakes on the job was extremely limited. His sons especially were expected to earn their keep, and any signs of laziness were dealt with by a swift box to the ear.

Illions set the pace in his shop by example. This was true not only of production but of perseverance. His son Rudy told the story of how his father, upon cutting his hand, would dip the cut into a nearby vat of hot glue, wrap a piece of cloth around it, and continue working. Since Illions's dexterity was such that he could carve just as well with either hand, this kind of injury would hardly slow his productivity.

Sometime after 1900, not far from the Illions shop, Charles Looff was hiring a young recently arrived Austrian immigrant carver by the name of John Zalar. As had been true of many of his contemporaries, Zalar's advancement in his carving abilities came through the creation of religious artifacts. Looff readily saw the talents exhibited by Zalar and soon had the young man creating a variety of carousel figures for his carousels.

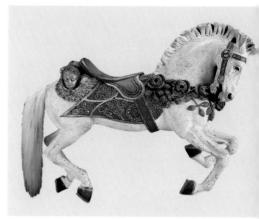

Although it is not known exactly when Zalar started his work for Looff, the look of Looff's animals changed dramatically around 1904. The features of his horses became softer, grew more animated, and took on a greater realism. And though it is unclear whether Zalar is the artistic hand behind this change, the figures that Zalar did create within this style are truly magnificent.

Zalar had what some describe as the gift of giving life to inanimate objects. There is a twinkle in the eye of a Zalar horse, the kind that makes you look twice to check that it didn't move when you glanced away. The poses are filled with vitality, yet the gentle faces invite the rider to climb up on the horse's back. Zalar's manes go from elegantly draped to wildly flying and everywhere in between. Zalar designed and expertly carved trappings using a vast array of motifs, from the Egyptian Sphinx to an English hunting party.

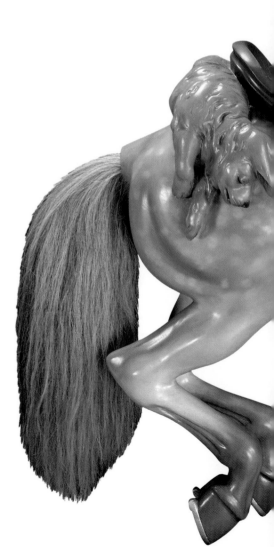

When Looff stopped making carousels in 1917, Zalar went to work for the Philadelphia Toboggan Company where he continued creating figures with a very similar style. Over the next seven years Zalar's health failed. He carved for as long as he could, eventually only working on the heads, until he died of tuberculosis at the age of fifty-one.

Daniel Müller's work as an artist goes well beyond the concept of creating a carousel figure. Even Salvatore Cernigliaro spoke in awe of this great sculptor, for when Müller's name was mentioned in a 1969 interview, he said, "Ah, Müller, there was a true artist." Because of his effect on this industry, his life is examined in greater detail in the next chapter.

FAR LEFT: THE EYES OF A ZALAR HORSE ALWAYS HAVE A CERTAIN SADNESS TO THEM, PERHAPS A REFLECTION OF THE CARVER'S HARD LIFE: HIS FIRST WIFE DIED VERY YOUNG, AND HE BATTLED CHRONIC TUBERCULOSIS. COLLECTION OF JOHN AND JAN DAVIS.

LEFT: EVEN IF ALL THE TRAPPINGS WERE REMOVED FROM A ZALAR HORSE, ONE WOULD STILL HAVE A WORK OF ART, AS IS EVIDENT FROM THIS LOOFF HORSE, C. 1914. COLLECTION OF JOHN AND CATHY DANIEL.

ABOVE: JOHN ZALAR WITH AN INSIDE-ROW FIGURE THAT HE CARVED FOR LOOFF, C. 1912.

DANIEL CARL MÜLLER:
THE CRAFTSMAN AS ARTIST

✳ ✳ ✳ ✳ ✳ ✳ ✳ ✳ ✳ ✳ ✳ ✳ ✳ ✳ ✳ ✳ ✳

CHAPTER 6

As the fledgling American carousel industry was taking its first steps in 1872, the third child of Johann Heinrich Müller was born in Hamburg, Germany. Throughout his early childhood, Daniel Carl Müller's life centered around his father and his father's skills as a designer and master cabinetmaker.

After corresponding with his friend Gustav Dentzel, the elder Müller decided that a better life awaited his family in America. So in 1881 Johann Müller took his wife, Wilhelmina, and three children, his younger son

INSETS: (TOP) FROM THE COLLECTION OF CHARLOTTE DINGER. (MIDDLE) FROM THE FREELS FOUNDATION COLLECTION. (BOTTOM) FROM THE COLLECTION OF JOHN AND CATHY DANIEL.

ALTHOUGH MOST OF THE ARTISTIC OUTPUT FELL INTO THE CATEGORY OF CAROUSEL ITEMS, DANIEL MÜLLER'S DESIRE, TALENT, AND ABILITY TO CREATE OTHER TYPES OF WORK ARE EVIDENT IN HIS SCULPTURE OF A MERMAID BALANCING A TURTLE IN HER HAIR. PHOTO: COURTESY OF EVELYN MULLER JOHNSON.

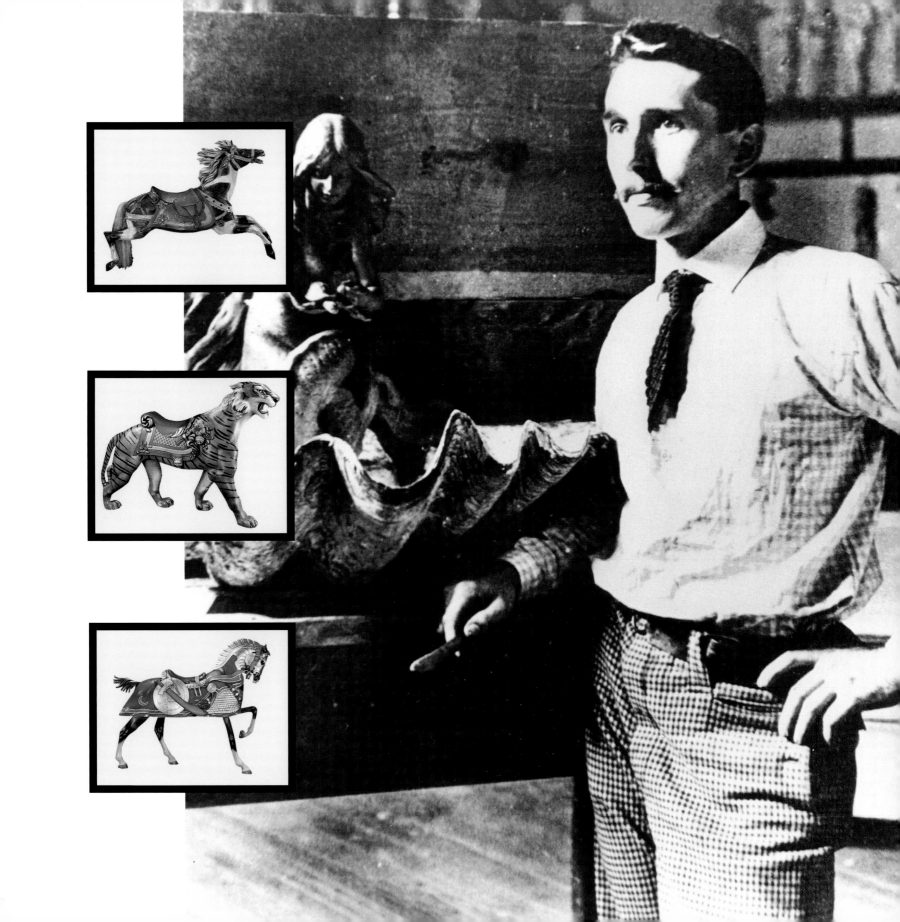

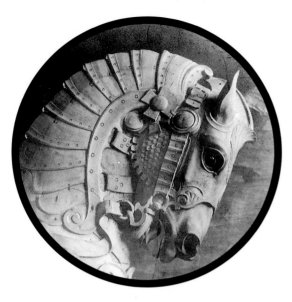

FACTORY PHOTOGRAPH, C. 1908, SHOWS A CLOSE-UP OF THE HEAD OF AN ARMORED MÜLLER HORSE. EVERY DETAIL OF THE FIGURE IS AN EXERCISE IN PRECISION CARVING, WITH EACH RIVET IN THE ARMOR RE-CREATED EXACTLY. UNFORTUNATELY, THE LOCATION OF THIS FIGURE IS UNKNOWN, AND IT HAS MOST LIKELY BEEN LOST OR DESTROYED. PHOTO: COURTESY OF SMITHSONIAN INSTITUTION.

Alfred, Daniel, and Daniel's older half-sister, Pauline, and joined the throngs of immigrants crossing the Atlantic Ocean, to set up household in the Gravesend district of Brooklyn. Johann's eldest son, Paul, chose to stay in Germany.

Acting on a suggestion made by Gustav, Johann Müller (who changed his name to John Miller) contacted Gustav's friendly rival Charles Looff about the possibility of a woodworking job. John was soon working in Looff's carousel factory, while Daniel and Alfred attended the local grade school during the morning and helped where they could at Looff's factory in the afternoons.

The hours at work were most likely filled with the tasks of most apprentice woodworkers. As an apprentice, a young boy would start out with the menial jobs of cleaning, sweeping, and following the orders of anyone else in the shop. Other tasks of greater responsibility would be added. One of the most important jobs was sharpening the tools. This took a steady hand and good eye since a very sharp, precisely beveled edge needed to be maintained on each tool. If a master carver felt that it was time to sharpen a chisel or gouge, it had to be done quickly and effectively or the apprentice would be told in no uncertain terms of his failure.

Only after years of menial jobs would the apprentice finally be allowed to begin working with wood. The new jobs would include mixing the hot hide glue and gluing together the basic forms, filling any knotholes that may have shown up during the carving process with plaster, and eventually roughing out some of the wooden bodies. Once an apprentice had mastered the use of the larger carving tools and had spent several years acquiring a feel for the grain and how the tools could move through the wood, he would be rewarded with a promotion to journeyman.

The Müller brothers were probably at this level when, in 1888, their father decided to move to Germantown, near Philadelphia. John Miller and his sons promptly went to work carving carousel figures for his old friend Gustav. Unfortunately, by the end of 1890, both John and Wilhelmina Müller had died. For his good friend, Gustav took over the rearing and tutelage of the two boys.

To enhance their careers, Daniel and Alfred enrolled at the Spring Garden Institute, a public art school in Philadelphia. For Daniel, who had a continual drive to improve his abilities, this was to be the start of twenty-three years of art classes. After studying at Spring Garden for two years, Daniel signed up for the

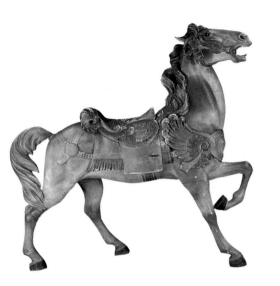

AN OUTSIDE-ROW STANDER DESIGNED BY DANIEL MÜLLER.
REELS FOUNDATION COLLECTION.

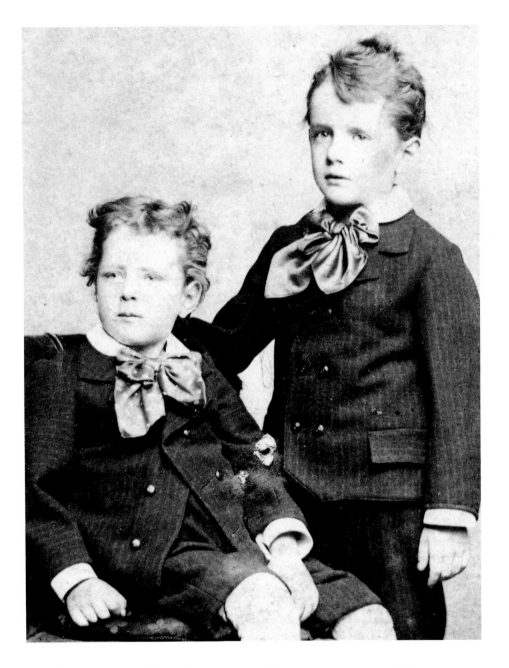

THE MÜLLER BROTHERS, DANIEL (RIGHT, AGE NINE) AND ALFRED (AGE SEVEN), JUST BEFORE
LEAVING HAMBURG, GERMANY. PHOTO: COURTESY OF EVELYN MULLER JOHNSON.

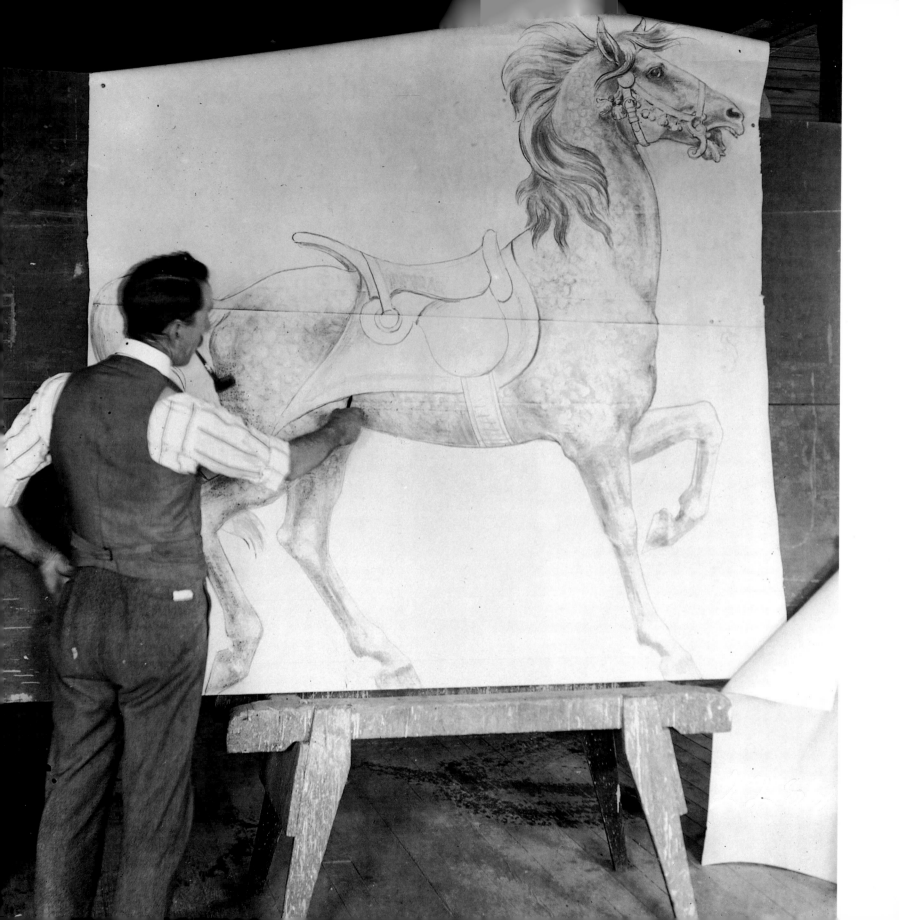

evening life drawing classes at the Pennsylvania Academy of the Fine Arts. It was there that, several years later, Daniel met the nationally known portrait sculptor Charles Grafly, who was to become his teacher, mentor, and friend for the next two decades.

In the 1890s, as Müller studied the fine arts at night, he spent his days creating carousel figures for his surrogate father, Gustav Dentzel. Since Daniel and Alfred's creative talents were enormous, Dentzel began to allow the Müllers a free hand at designing figures. This led not only to the development of many of the menagerie figures, including roosters, cats, rabbits, ostriches, and the rare sea horse, but to a more realistic and decorative look. During this period Daniel Müller met and married Elizabeth Muhe.

Gustav Dentzel was a stern man, and he felt that all his boys, including the Müllers, needed to be guided by a heavy hand. Eventually Daniel and Alfred tired of this treatment and in 1899 left the employ of Dentzel. Dentzel felt that if these young men had so little respect for his authority, then they would no longer be welcome in the Dentzel shop, ever.

Fortunately for the Müllers, around this time Henry Auchy and his partners were negotiating with carousel maker E. Joy Morris to purchase the remainder of his stock of wooden figures. This was the beginning of what was soon to become the carousel and roller coaster manufacturer Philadelphia Toboggan Company, and Auchy was looking for skilled carvers to build carousels for him. The designs that Daniel Müller created for the Philadelphia Toboggan Company set the carving style for that company for the next ten years. This meant that almost every carousel that came out of the Philadelphia area between 1900 and 1907 was heavily influenced by the artistic hand of Daniel Müller.

The Müllers worked exclusively for Auchy for three years until they were approached by a young business-minded man named Patrick Kilcullen.

THE SIDE OF THIS HORSE CARRIES THE TRADITIONAL DENTZEL DECORATION OF AN EAGLE CLUTCHING A FLAG USED BY THE DENTZEL COMPANY FROM 1904 UNTIL THE COMPANY CLOSED IN 1927. BUT THIS HORSE WITH A WONDERFUL MÜLLER-CARVED HEAD IS THE ONLY ONE OF ITS KIND KNOWN. COLLECTION OF JOHN AND CATHY DANIEL.

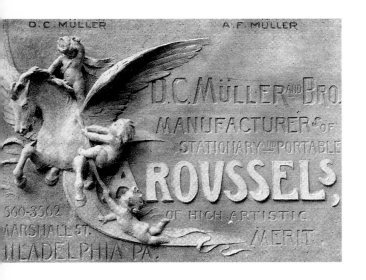

MÜLLER CREATED A SPECTACULAR CARVING IN RELIEF, WHICH HE THEN HAD PHOTOGRAPHED AND TURNED INTO HIS BUSINESS CARD. PHOTO: COURTESY OF EVELYN MULLER JOHNSON.

Kilcullen had a strong entrepreneurial spirit and convinced the brothers to start their own company. In 1902 both D. C. Müller and Bro. and the U.S. Caroussell and Amusement Company were formed. D. C. Müller and Bro. was organized to design and build the carousels that would then be placed and operated by the second company. While the day-to-day business side of the U.S. Caroussell Company was handled by Kilcullen, the creative side was in the Müllers' hands. That first year was a hectic one, as their goal was to have two full carousels up and running by the summer of 1903.

The Müller shop was small, but the carving staff was quite talented. Several Dentzel carvers jumped ship and worked for the Müllers exclusively, while others, such as Cernigliaro, would moonlight (unknown to Gustav) for Daniel when orders were slow at the Dentzel shop. Of those who came to work for the Müllers on a full-time basis, Ernst Kraus and Charles Leopold were the most talented and dedicated.

Müller continued creating figures for the Philadelphia Toboggan Company until 1907 when the company decided to bring most of its carving in-house. But by this time, Müller had a steady list of clients and six carousels operating under the umbrella of the U.S. Caroussell and Amusement Company. Times were good. The only thing seeming to hold the company back was the rate of production. Daniel was a perfectionist, and even the slogan on his business card, "Carrousels of High Artistic Merit" alluded to the detail and sculptural expertise that went into a Müller carousel. This adherence to detail must have fulfilled Daniel's need to express the artist within him. It also must have frustrated Kilcullen's business sense, for the company never prospered to the degree of Dentzel or the Philadelphia Toboggan Company.

In 1909 Gustav Dentzel died. He had never forgiven the Müller boys for taking their leave without his permission, but the grudge did not go past the father. When William Dentzel took over the family business it wasn't long before Müller-style horses were offered as an option on a new Dentzel carousel. The 1914 Dentzel carousel at the Texas State Fair is filled with figures designed and carved at the Müller shop.

Daniel continued to take his evening art classes through 1913, ever striving to improve his abilities. But despite some of his earlier works, such as the mermaid sculpture that he created at the Pennsylvania Academy of the Fine Arts, he never

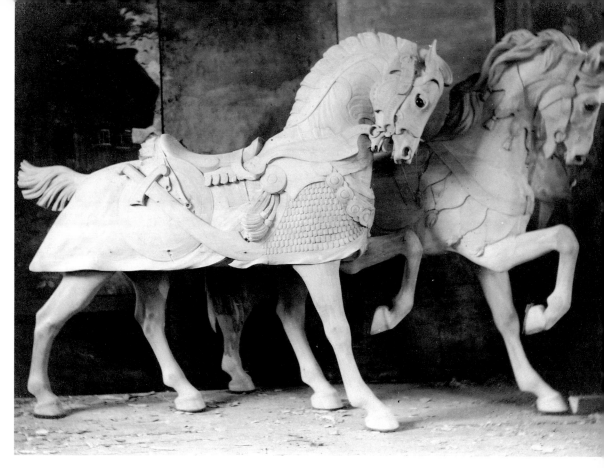

pursued the career of fine art sculptor. Whether it was by artistic choice or just the need to make a living, his creative talents were channeled into the art of the carousel. Through this medium of the amusement industry, Daniel Müller created masterpieces of strength and motion, gallant steeds captured in a wooden frame. There was no sound business reason for Müller to carve stitching holes in some of the saddles or for him to finish the face of a tiny eagle carved on the scabbard of a sword. The detail and exacting muscular tones of his horses did not sell any more tickets or persuade someone new to ride the carousel. All of these aspects were added because this was his art.

For the Müllers, the dream of business ownership ended fifteen years after it began. The Great War turned the public's attention away from the manufacture of carousels, and in 1917 D. C. Müller and Bro. closed its doors for good. Most of the carvers, including the Müllers, went back to work at the Dentzel Company. This was where they continued to produce carousels until 1928, when William Dentzel died and the remainder of the Dentzel factory was sold to the Philadelphia Toboggan Company. The age of carousel carving had largely come to a close by then. Daniel and Alfred did piece work when they could by repairing or embellishing existing carousels, but the work was sporadic. Daniel designed and built a house in Brigantine, New Jersey, where, over the next number of years, he enjoyed many days fishing with his good friend Harry Dentzel. But the hours spent creating his marvelous wooden animals were no more.

The last years were spent in his home in Northfield, New Jersey. In 1952, at the age of seventy-nine, Daniel Müller died. He was not to know that the legacy of carving which he left behind would find the enormous appreciation that it has today.

ABOVE: A RARE MÜLLER ARMORED HORSE, c. 1912, SHOWN IN THE FACTORY. PHOTO: COURTESY OF SMITHSONIAN INSTITUTION.

BELOW: ONE OF THE MAIN INSPIRATIONS IN THE CREATION OF MÜLLER'S CAROUSEL HORSES WAS THE U.S. CALVALRY. THE CONGRESSIONAL MEDAL OF HONOR ON THE SIDE OF THIS HORSE, c. 1910, REFERS TO THE ALL-BLACK CALVARY DIVISION, ONE OF THE MOST HIGHLY DECORATED DIVISIONS IN THE ENTIRE MILITARY. COLLECTION OF JOHN AND CATHY DANIEL.

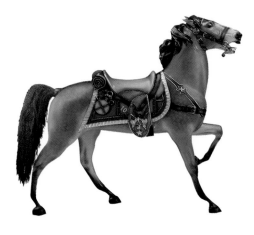

LOSS AND REDISCOVERY

❀ ❀ ❀ ❀ ❀ ❀ ❀ ❀ ❀ ❀ ❀ ❀ ❀ ❀ ❀ ❀ ❀

CHAPTER 7

The craftsmen whose livelihoods had depended on the Industrial Revolution could only stand by and watch as technology began to eat away at their own jobs. The same labor-saving inventions that had helped to create the leisure time of the weekend were now being used to produce rides and even to carve carousel figures.

The basic design of a carving (or duplicating) machine has been around since 1900 and was used in a limited way by many of the carousel manufacturers to rough out basic

WHEN A TRAVELING CARNIVAL WENT OUT OF BUSINESS, MANY OF THE RIDES WERE SOLD OR PLACED IN STORAGE. THE CAROUSELS FROM THESE FAIRS OCCASIONALLY WERE "TEMPORARILY" STORED IN A NEARBY BARN WHERE THEY SAT FOR YEARS. THIS C. 1890 NORMAN AND EVANS CAROUSEL WAS DISCOVERED IN A BARN OUTSIDE KANSAS CITY IN 1985. IT WAS BOUGHT AND RESTORED BY DON AND RUTH SNYDER AND IS CURRENTLY OPERATING IN THE KANSAS CITY AREA. PHOTO: COURTESY OF JOHN DANIEL.

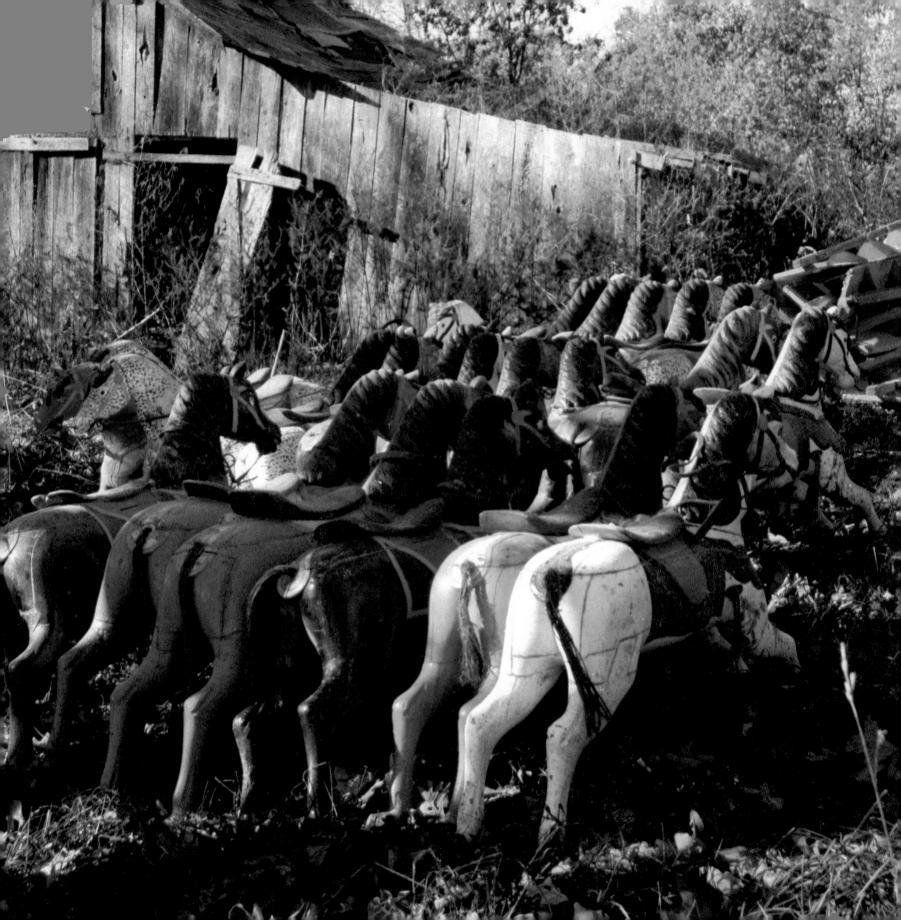

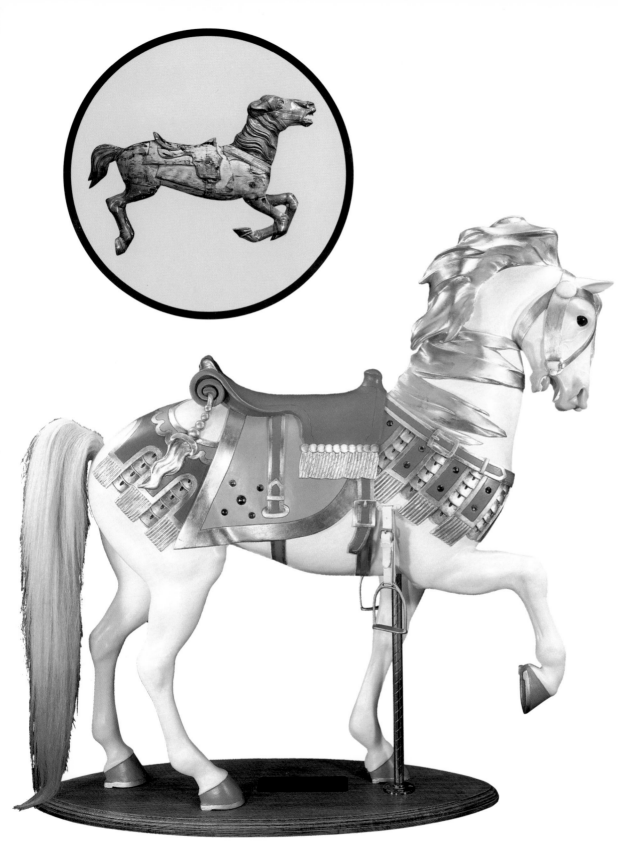

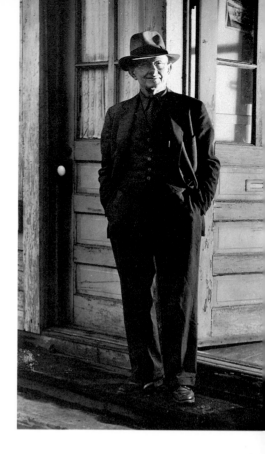

ABOVE: Marcus Charles Illions outside his small Brooklyn office in the late 1940s. Illions never gave up hope that the carousel would make a comeback. Unfortunately, it would not happen in his lifetime, but his sons, Rudy and Barney, did witness the revival of the carousel's popularity. Photo: courtesy of Bernard and Bette Illions.

TOP LEFT: The use of metal in the construction of carousel horses signaled the end of the wooden horse. Here, an Allan Herschell Compahy horse is shown with aluminum head, legs, and tail, c. 1930.

LEFT: A beautifully restored M. C. Illions horse, c. 1914. Corey Collection.

RIGHT: This carving machine could produce four identical bodies based on the original piece, located in the center. It works on a principle similar to a key duplicating machine, which follows the pattern of the master key in reproducing a matching key. Photo: courtesy of Smithsonian Institution.

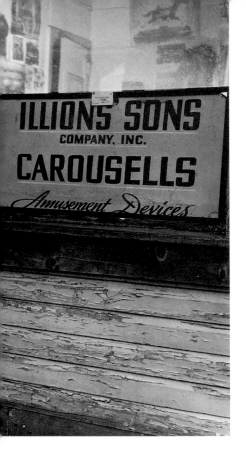

shapes from a variety of master patterns. But after the wood had been routered down to an approximate size, it was still up to the carver to add detail, to make the mane fall gently down the neck or appear to swirl with the wind. As the carving machines became more sophisticated, there was less and less for the carvers to do. The owners of many companies then realized that they could lower their costs and become more competitive by simplifying their designs so that they were more compatible with the carving machines.

In addition, the Allan Herschell Company started experimenting with casting aluminum in the mid-1920s, first just for the legs, then for heads, and finally for the entire body. The more durable and less expensive cast-metal horses were the wave of the future for carousel manufacturing and would be the dominant form of production for the next forty years.

If these new aspects of technology had not finished off the hand craftsman, the economy certainly did. Although the demand for carousels had started to slip during World War I, the onset of the Depression stopped it altogether. By 1932, when the Philadelphia Toboggan Company was setting up the last brand new wooden carousel in Asbury Park, New Jersey, Dentzel, Illions, and Carmel had already gone out of business. Both Stein and Goldstein and Looff's family members were concentrating on running their amusement parks and concessions, while the makers of traveling carousels had switched to the cast-aluminum method.

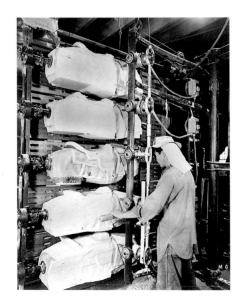

The carvers who had spent most of their lives creating a stable of marvelous wooden creatures were now relegated to repair and touch-up work. Daniel Müller landed a brief job recarving the trappings on a Dentzel carousel at Cedar Point Amusement Park in Ohio. For a while Marcus Charles Illions stayed busy repairing his Coney Island machines, but one by one, the places that owned his carousels closed down. Salvatore Cernigliaro eventually left for California where he taught art, while Frank Carretta stayed on at the Philadelphia Toboggan Company carving casting patterns and filling in at odd jobs. Work for these master craftsmen was extremely scarce.

The carousels themselves did not fare much better. They were made of wood, and wood ages. It swells and shrinks with a change in the weather, it reacts to heat and cold and is subject to fungus infestation leading to dry rot, not to mention being on the lunch menu for termites. Glue joints give out, and the carver's exacting detail is subject to the abrasion of hundreds of thousands of feet that have urged their wooden steeds to go ever faster.

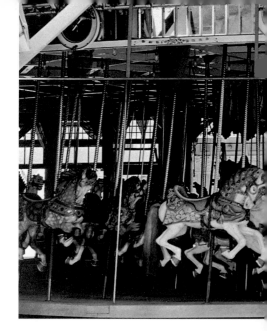

Looking to increase attendance, amusement park operators brought in more daring and technologically advanced rides. Carousels became the staid, older rides, needing more and more attention and maintenance as the machinery and figures aged. Many operators did not have the time or money to carefully replace legs and ears, so nails, bolts, old tin cans—anything that was close at hand—were used to make the necessary repairs.

Some carousels never even had a chance to deteriorate. The bane of amusement parks was fire. The entire park was usually put together with wood lath, nails, plaster, and tar. Electric wiring was liberally strung throughout to give the place that magical, lit up feeling at night. Unfortunately, this led to the park lighting up in the wrong way. Almost every major amusement complex in the country that was built before the 1940s has had at least one fire. In many cases, the carousel would end up as one of the victims.

But forty years after the last Philadelphia Toboggan Company carousel was placed, a strange and wonderful thing started happening. People began discovering their roots, all kinds of roots. They began to rediscover a sense of cultural heritage, craftsmanship, and design and combined that discovery with a general nostalgia for the "good old days." Many items once tossed on the junk heaps of America were being reexamined. Quilts and weather vanes, Shaker furniture and cigar store Indians, and, of course, carousel animals were being dug of out barns and attics and seen anew. People would scratch their heads with amazement when they realized that many of these items were "handmade," a concept that had been lost somewhere along the line. They started looking around for the people who had created these unique parts of our historical heritage and were deeply dismayed to find that almost all of them were gone.

Fortunately, author and historian Frederick Fried had the foresight to write about the intrinsic value of carousels and spent years interviewing the few remaining carvers and documenting the information that was swiftly disappearing. Published in 1964, Fried's book, *A Pictorial History of the Carousel,* quickly became the reference source for carousel fans.

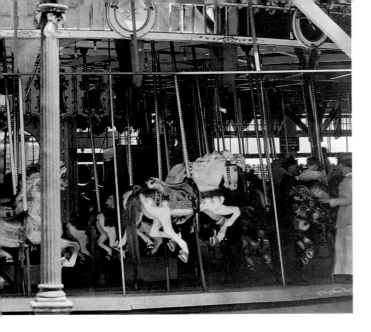

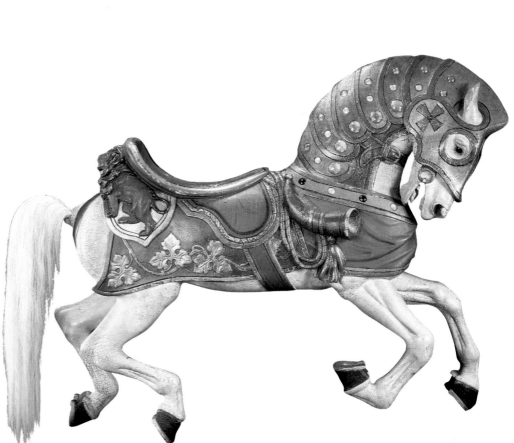

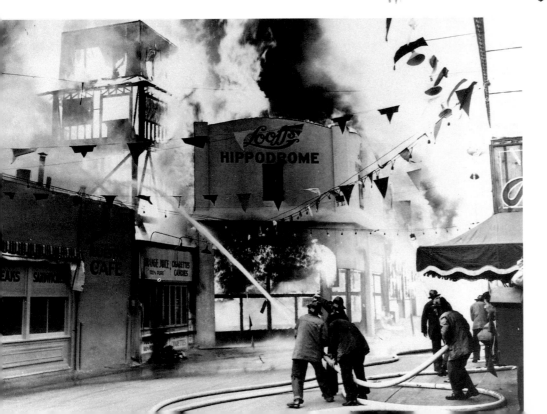

ABOVE LEFT: A Looff carousel located in the Hippodrome at the Pike in Long Beach, California. Photo: courtesy of Willie Looff Taucher.

ABOVE RIGHT: This armored horse was in the paint shop at the time of the fire and was the lone survivor of the 1943 fire. Collection of Roland and Jo Summit.

LEFT: Looff's Hippodrome burning to the ground in a 1943 fire. Photo: courtesy of Al Brown.

Nine years later a small group of enthusiasts came together to form the National Carousel Roundtable (renamed the National Carousel Association). Their first convention was held at the Heritage Plantation Museum in Sandwich, Massachusetts, and it seemed to them that the entire world had shown up. Over 200 people with a similar interest in this esoteric piece of the American past had gathered to talk, show pictures, and share their experiences. No one there realized that their enthusiasm would soon spread, eventually touching hundreds of thousands of people across the country.

Since that day in 1973, half a dozen books have been published, hundreds of articles have been written, carousel magazines have sprung up, and thousands of gift items depicting carousels and carousel figures have appeared in stores around the world, not to mention calendars, note cards, and a myriad of other products.

The main beneficiary of all of this attention has been carousels. Amusement parks that still have the original wooden carousels have come to view them, not as old clunkers of a ride, but as true pieces of Americana that are well worth restoring and highlighting as a draw to the public.

Both Disneyland and Disney World have put their carousels in showplace spots right next to Sleeping Beauty's Castle, while smaller, family-owned parks like Sea Breeze in Rochester, New York, have painstakingly restored their machines, displaying them as the gem of the park. Cities such as Spokane, Washington, and Meridian, Mississippi, have taken a great deal of public pride in the operation and maintenance of their machines, and carousels are appearing more and more as centerpieces in shopping malls.

So why all the fuss? The ingredients that go into the universal love of carousels are definitely unique. No other aspect of our heritage can claim to combine the nostalgia, innocence, and fantasy of childhood with the romantic history of renaissance France, the innovations of the Industrial Revolution, and the exquisitely talented craftsmen of turn-of-the-century America. The carousel, with its menagerie of hand-carved figures, has etched a place not only in our history but in our hearts.

One would be hard-pressed to find a person who has not spent a few minutes of his or her life whirling around in a happy daze aboard a wooden steed. This wondrous machine has cut across all boundaries by entertaining everyone, no matter what religion or background, class or age. It is clear that the carousel has become an object of joy through the ages and for all ages.

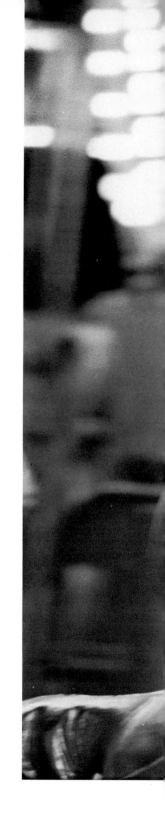

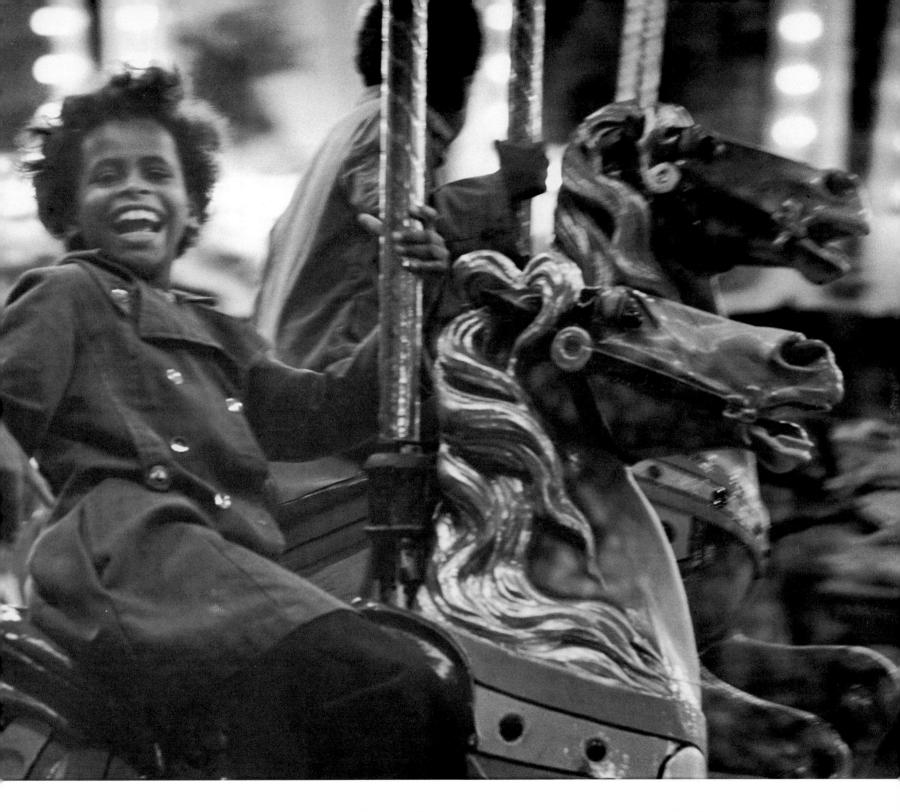

A YOUNG RIDER ENJOYS A MOMENT ABOARD A PORTABLE PHILADELPHIA TOBOGGAN COMPANY CAROUSEL. PHOTO: COURTESY OF BARBARA FAHS CHARLES.

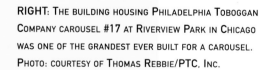

RIGHT: THE BUILDING HOUSING PHILADELPHIA TOBOGGAN COMPANY CAROUSEL #17 AT RIVERVIEW PARK IN CHICAGO WAS ONE OF THE GRANDEST EVER BUILT FOR A CAROUSEL. PHOTO: COURTESY OF THOMAS REBBIE/PTC, INC.

ABOVE: THE IDYLLIC SCENE WAS ENHANCED BY THE STRINGS OF LIGHTS AND THE DEPICTION OF ANGELS CAVORTING AROUND THE CORNICE OF THE CAROUSEL. PHOTO: COURTESY OF THOMAS REBBIE/PTC, INC.

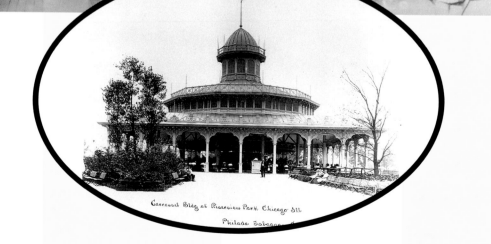

Carousel Bldg at Riverview Park, Chicago, Ill.

Philada. Toboggan

PHILADELPHIA TOBOGGAN COMPANY CAROUSEL #17

The idea was to build the grandest amusement park in the country west of New York's Coney Island. In 1903 construction began on Riverview Park, just outside of Chicago.

To suit such a magnificent park, the builders looked for an equally marvelous carousel. They chose the Philadelphia Toboggan Company to design and build an enormous seventy-horse, four-chariot, five-abreast carousel to be housed in a great four-story structure that was to be the centerpiece of the entire park.

The carousel was installed in time for opening day in 1908, and for the next fifty-nine years, Riverview Park and the Philadelphia Toboggan Company carousel #17 entertained millions of patrons from around the world. If one mentions Riverview Park to natives of Chicago, they will surely offer a string of wonderful memories of perfect summer days spent wandering among the rides.

In 1967, the economics of declining attendance forced the park to close its gates forever. The fate of the carousel was uncertain until the Six Flags Corporation bought Philadelphia Toboggan Company carousel #17 for installation at their new park, Six Flags Over Georgia, located just outside of Atlanta. In order to house the carousel properly, they even built a replica of the carousel building at Riverview Park. Since 1971, thanks to Six Flags, the carousel has continued to entertain tens of thousands of joyous riders each summer.

CAROUSEL DOCTORS

❋ ❋ ❋ ❋ ❋ ❋ ❋ ❋ ❋ ❋ ❋ ❋ ❋ ❋ ❋ ❋

CHAPTER 8

Before they were rediscovered, carousels led a rather humble existence. Many carousel owners considered the animals merely seats on an amusement park ride, a way of generating profit, while others did not have the means to properly restore their rides. Since the purpose of a carousel was primarily functional rather than aesthetic, repairs to the animals were often done haphazardly. Eventually, decades of makeshift repairs and multiple coats of "park" paint (paint applied by the owner or operator), along with the wear and tear of tens of thousands of riders, took their toll on the detail of the finely crafted individual figures.

REMOVING LAYERS OF PAINT WITH A COLD STRIPPING PROCESS AT BIC'S FURNITURE STRIPPING.

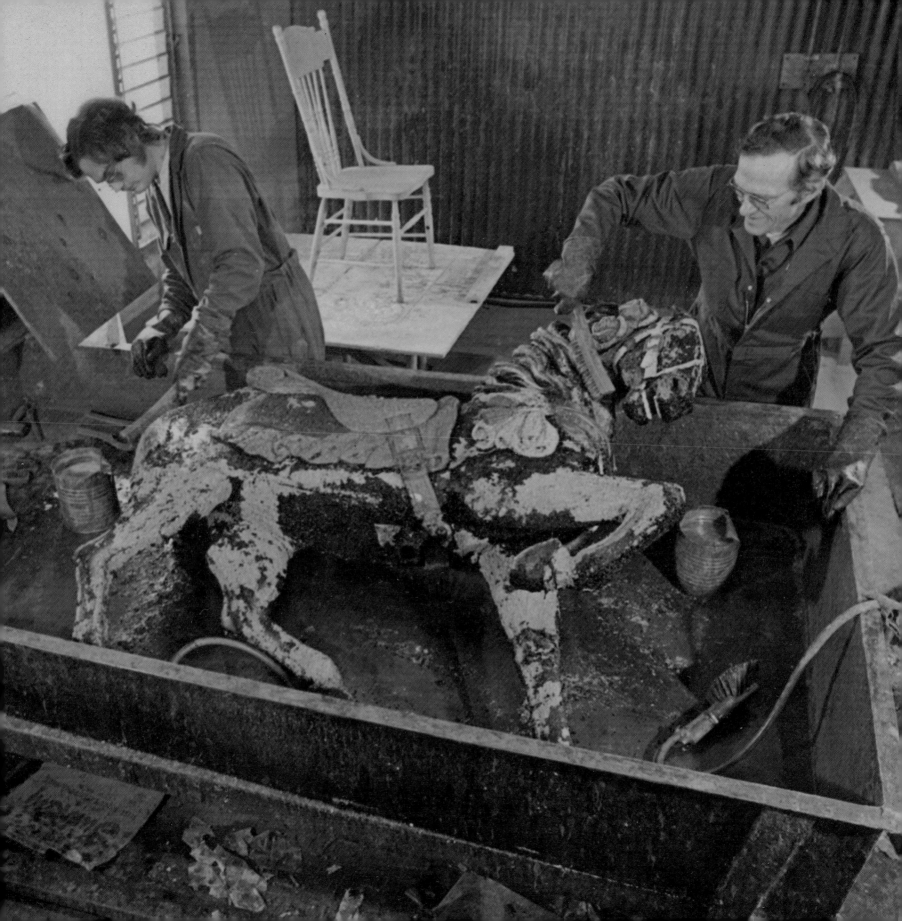

It wasn't until the late 1960s, when carousels first recaptured the attention of enthusiasts, that people recognized a need to rehabilitate these ailing animals. In the restoration process, a carousel "doctor" tries to undo all the unintended damage that has occurred over the years. In the conservation process, the conservator hopes to retard any ongoing damage to the figure, stabilize the wood, and maintain the figure with as little physical change as possible. And considering the fact that the youngest carousels are now more than sixty years old, there's often a lot of work to do. In most cases, completely restoring a carousel can take up to eight months, with an individual figure requiring anywhere from thirty to several hundred hours, depending on how ornate and badly damaged the animal is

When an animal is brought in for "treatment," the restorer or conservator's first job is to evaluate its overall condition without removing the paint. This can be difficult, since a coat of paint often hides a multitude of sins. Animals that look "healthy" on the outside may turn out to be in bad shape once the layers of paint have been peeled away. On the other hand, figures that look ragged on the outside may actually be in good condition on the inside. In most cases, the paint must be stripped off in order to tell how much restoration work the figure needs.

Next, the restorer determines if the animal's original factory paint is still intact beneath the many layers of park paint. (Over the years, an animal may have accumulated twenty, thirty, or even forty coats—up to one-eighth of an inch in

THE PROCESS OF PAINTING A DENTZEL TIGER IS SHOWN IN SIX STAGES

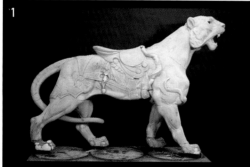

BARE WOOD READY TO PAINT.

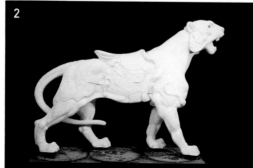

A BASE COAT OF THICK WHITE PAINT.

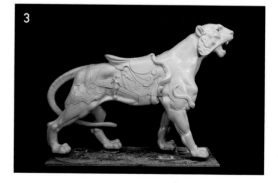

AN UNDERCOAT OF BASIC TIGER COLOR.

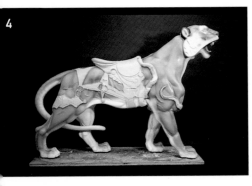

FINISHED BODY COLOR WITH A BEGINNING OF COLORS ON THE TRAPPINGS.

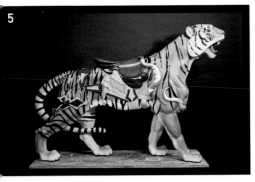

STRIPES ARE MOSTLY FINISHED AND THE TRAPPINGS ARE CLOSE TO COMPLETION.

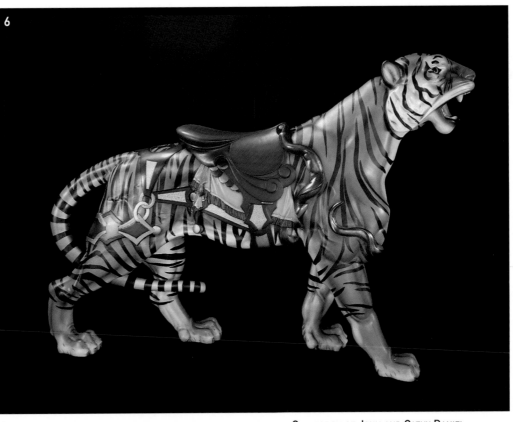

THE FINAL PAINT WITH AN ANTIQUING GLAZE AND A COAT OF VARNISH. COLLECTION OF JOHN AND CATHY DANIEL.

thickness.) Rosa Ragan, a carousel restorer in North Carolina, accomplishes this task by carefully scraping away a small, unobtrusive patch of paint using a scalpel and a blow dryer. If the original paint is still in place, its highly detailed and decorative style is easy to distinguish from hastily applied park paint. Many times, however, the restorer discovers that the original paint has long since been removed or isn't worth salvaging, in which case the animal is stripped down to the bare wood. Now the real work begins.

Originally, carousel animals were fashioned from numerous pieces of wood and assembled with only wooden dowels and glue. In order to return an animal to its former glory, the restorer must remove all "foreign objects," such as nuts, bolts, nails, screws, and metal patches, and redo the repairs properly. This process involves cutting out rotted sections of wood, building up worn or abraded areas, and, in some cases, replacing an entire hoof, ear, leg, or tail.

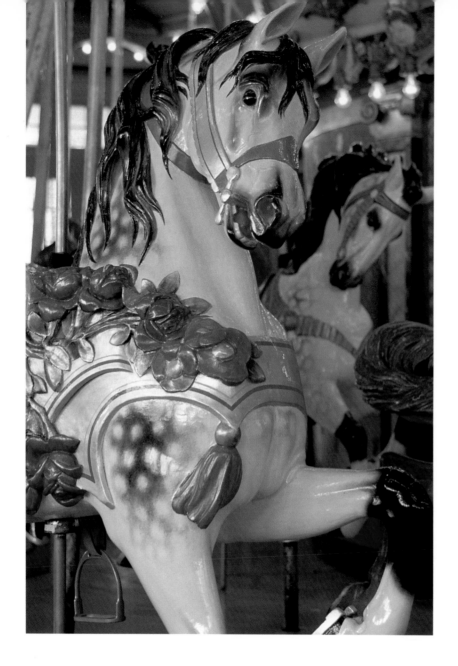

Ornate animals that have been heavily abraded are among the most difficult figures to restore. On these animals, fine details—such as the face of a cherub or the flowers on a saddle—must be meticulously built back up and recarved in the original style. How does a restorer know what the animal looked like originally? Experience. Without seeing the rest of the animal, a well-versed carousel restorer can look at a single hoof, ear, tail, or eye and determine who the carver was and approximately when the figure was made. That's how distinctive each manufacturer's style was.

Figures produced for traveling carnivals by manufacturers like Charles W. Parker and Allan Herschell often require the most extensive repair work, according to Will Morton VIII, a carousel conservator and restorer in Colorado. Because these animals were carted around in trucks and not protected from the elements, they were more likely to sustain damage than animals produced for permanent carousels by manufacturers like the Dentzel Company and the Philadelphia Toboggan Company.

Once all of the damage to the wood has been repaired, the animal is primed, sanded, and readied for repainting. If the figure is part of a private collection, and the valuable original paint is still intact, Ragan simply touches up the paint and applies a coat of clear varnish to the animal. If the figure is part of an operating carousel, however, she covers the varnish with several coats of fresh paint so that the original isn't damaged by the riders.

The animal can either be repainted in its original color style or in an entirely new color scheme. Each option has its merits. Repainting in original style preserves the vision and artistry of the original maker. Updated color schemes often reflect the personal taste of the painter or owner and can be used to enhance the sculptural aspects of the figure.

Repainting with tube oil paints can take several weeks to complete. Each coat of oil paint must dry overnight, and the animal may have to receive three coats of body color and up to four coats of color for the trappings. Some restorers coat the figure with an antiquing glaze for an aged appearance, then top it with varnish to protect it from humidity and temperature changes.

After weeks of painstaking stripping, carving, priming, sanding, and repainting, the carousel animal has been transformed from its worn, weather-beaten condition back to its original beauty. At times this transformation is so dramatic that many restorers can't help feeling that they've brought the animals back to life—to a life in which they are once again fully appreciated, valued, and ridden with a new respect for the artists who created these masterpieces of the midway.

OCCASIONALLY A CAROUSEL MANUFACTURER WOULD USE A VARIETY OF WOODS TO CREATE A FIGURE SUCH AS THIS INSIDE-ROW DENTZEL JUMPER.

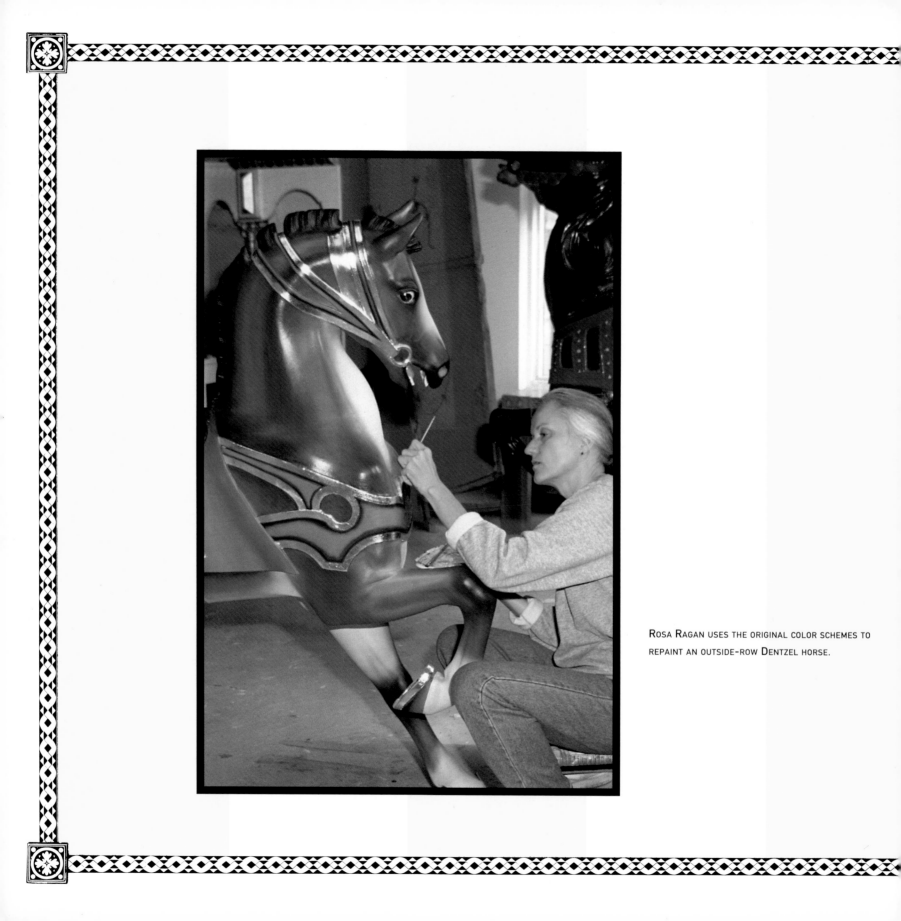

ROSA RAGAN USES THE ORIGINAL COLOR SCHEMES TO
REPAINT AN OUTSIDE-ROW DENTZEL HORSE.

ROSA RAGAN

In 1978, Rosa Ragan decided to begin a new career after losing her job as an art teacher in Raleigh, North Carolina. When a freind asked her what she wanted to do, Ragan responded that she wanted to be "some sort of an art conservator." A week later, she was asked to volunteer at a project to restore an entire Dentzel carousel at Pullen Park in Raleigh.

"All of the animals had to be cleaned down to the original paint. And there were four, five, six layers of paint. It sounded impossible to me," she recalls. "I talked to furniture restorers and they said they wouldn't touch it with a ten-foot pole." Motivated by the challenge, Ragan took on the job, working alone for an entire first year before completing the project with a staff of ten. The experience inspired her to spend a month visiting carousels and amusement parks in West Virginia, Ohio, Michigan, New York, and Canada. "That trip sealed my fate. That was the big transition for me," she says.

When Ragan returned home, she began working on a second carousel in Raleigh and launched her own carousel restoration business. Today, she's one of the busiest and most sought-after conservators in the industry. Yet, she remains a one-woman operation. "I don't want to be a bigger shop. I don't want to be a manager. I want to do the work," she says. "People tell me I would make more money if I expanded, but that's not what I'm interested in. I feel really lucky that I've found something I love to do."

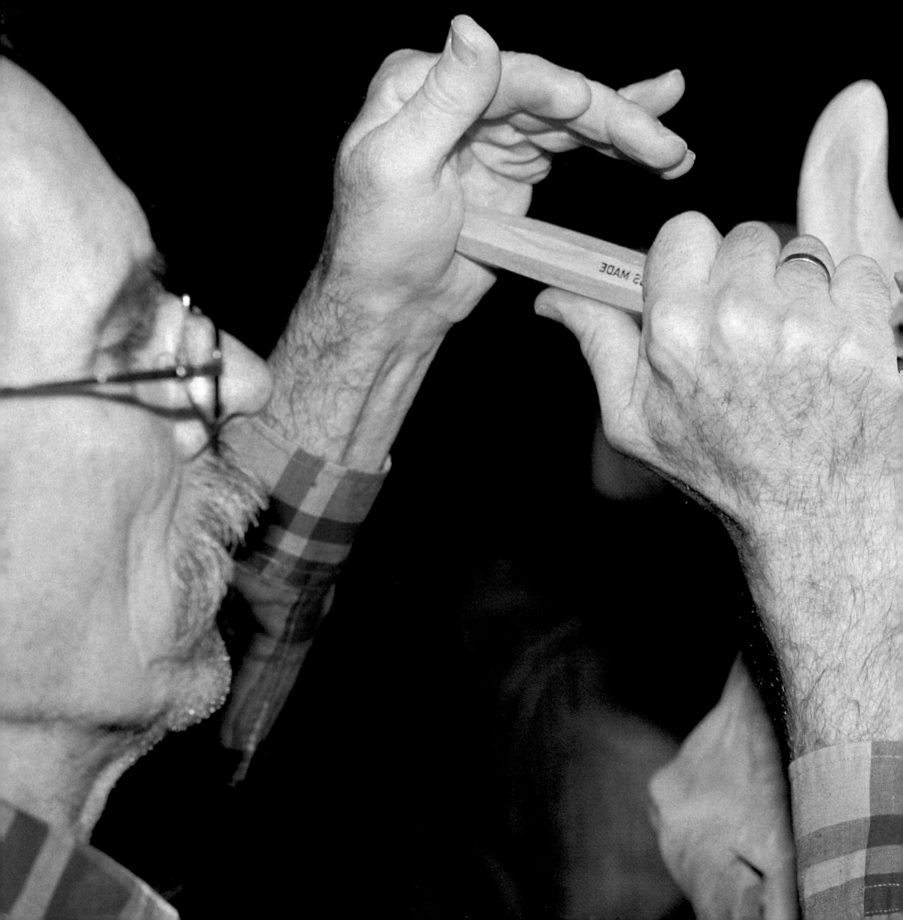

WILL MORTON

While working as a sculptor back in 1976, Will Morton agreed to help an associate's father restore the fory-five oil paintings on the inner panels of a Philadelphia Toboggan Company carousel at the county fairgrounds in Burlington, Colorado. As it turned out, however, his partner became ill during the early stages of the project, and Morton ended up doing the majority of the work. As a result, the volunteer committee that operates the carousel tapped Morton to restore all forty-six animals.

"Those were the dark ages of carousel restoration. People were just starting to get into it and didn't know much about it," he recalls. "During those first few years I worked really hard to learn everything I could about carousels and restoration. The upshot is that I'm still in the business today."

Despite the fact that Morton considers carousel restoration to be "hard and tedious," he still gets a charge out of it after all these years. "Working with paint is like being a detective. You discover all kinds of things as you remove the layers and take the animals apart," he says. "You find designs underneath the paint. You find lines that show you where to glue blocks of wood. You find scribbles that say 'front' or 'left.' There it is, penciled in the carver's own handwriting, as clearly as if he had written it yesterday."

For Morton, who has restored entire carousels in Colorado, Kansas, and New York, one of the biggest challenges is avoiding the temptation to tamper with the original artist's work. "I have to slap my hand all the time so that I don't make corrections," he laughs. "It's very difficult for a creative person to do restoration because you always want to change things—just a little bit."

MORTON CARVES A REPLACEMENT SECTION OF THE MANE ON
A HORSE FROM THE CHARLES CARMEL CAROUSEL IN
PROSPECT PARK, BROOKLYN, NEW YORK.

OLD METHODS, NEW ANIMALS

❀ ❀ ❀ ❀ ❀ ❀ ❀ ❀ ❀ ❀ ❀ ❀ ❀ ❀ ❀ ❀ ❀

CHAPTER 9

Shuffling around in their cluttered workshops, with wood chips blanketing the floor and dust clinging to their hair, Joe Leonard, Gerry Holzman, and Bill Finkenstein look more like run-of-the-mill woodworkers than visionaries responsible for ushering in a new era in the history of the carousel. But looks can be deceiving. And in the case of Leonard, Holzman, and Finkenstein, they definitely are. These three talented carvers have picked up where Daniel Müller and his peers left off more than sixty years ago and have revived the art of the hand-carved carousel animal.

A FEW OF THE CARVED ANIMALS ARE ON DISPLAY IN HOLZMAN'S WORKSHOP AWAITING THE COMPLETION OF THE EMPIRE STATE CAROUSEL.

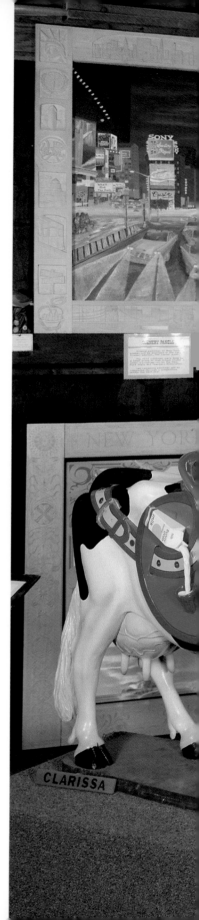

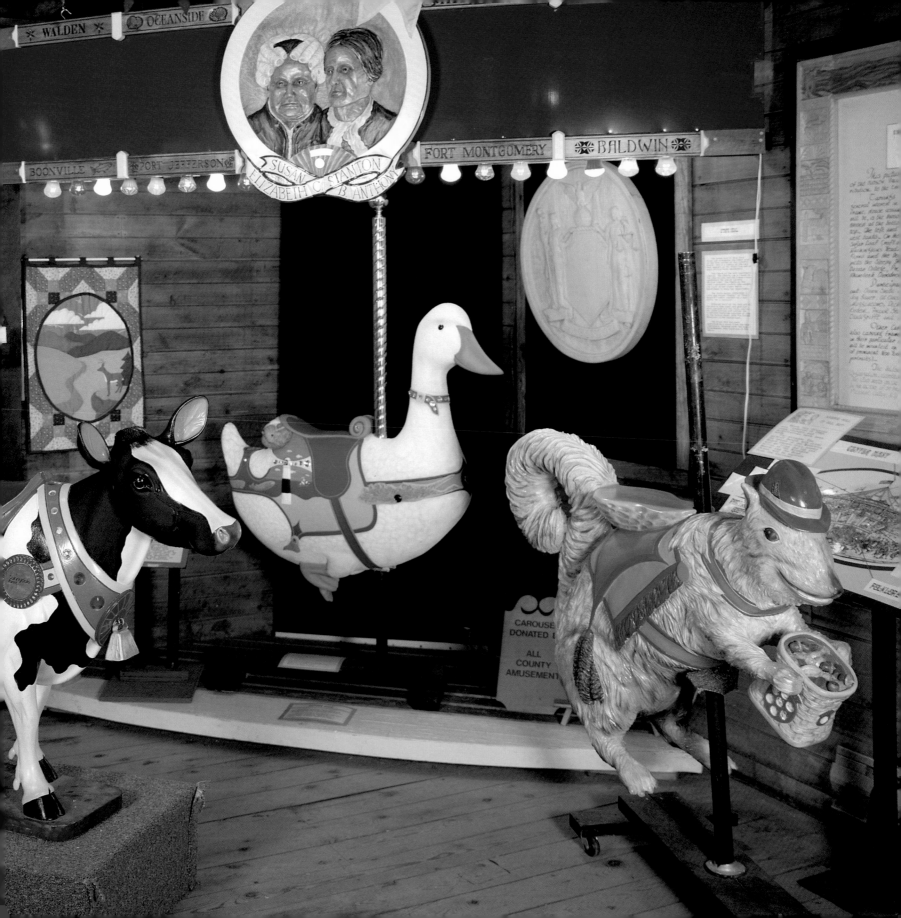

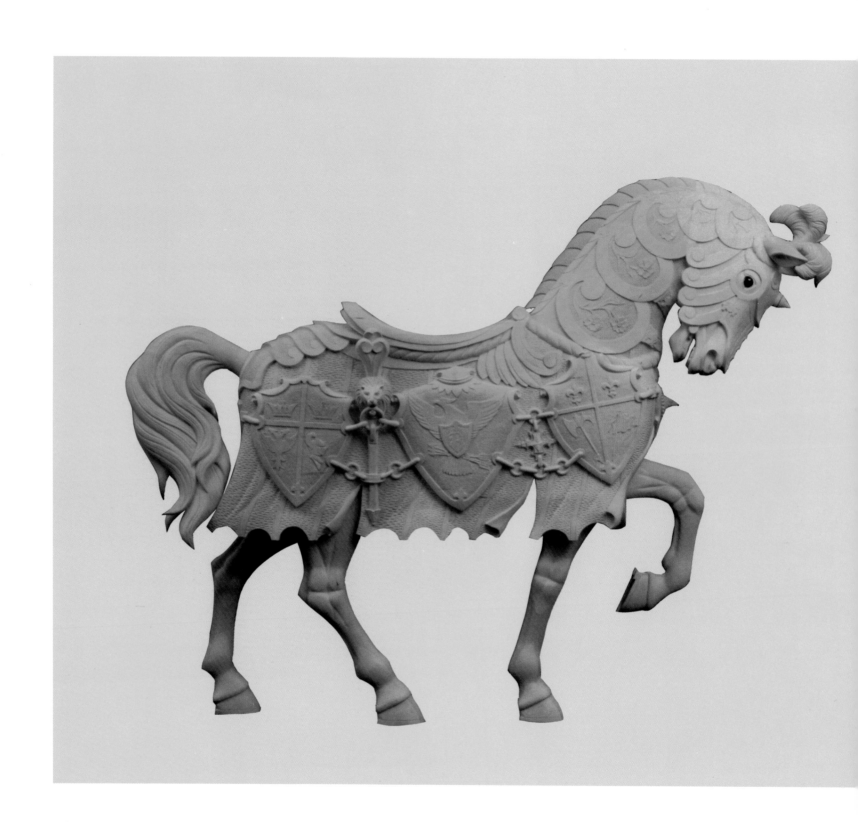

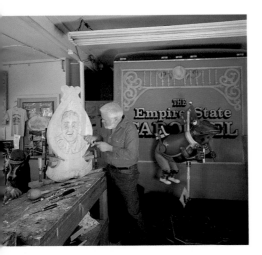

ABOVE: GERRY HOLZMAN WORKING ON A SHIELD FOR THE EMPIRE STATE CAROUSEL. THE PORTRAIT IS THAT OF FORMER NEW YORK CITY MAYOR, FIORELLO LA GUARDIA.

LEFT: ONE OF THE LARGE OUTSIDE-ROW ARMORED HORSES DESIGNED AND CARVED FOR THE EURO-DISNEY CAROUSEL BY JOE LEONARD.

Leonard, owner of Custom Woodcarving in Garrettsville, Ohio, has been restoring and carving carousel animals for the past seventeen years. He "fell into" the business when a customer walked into his advertising studio and asked him to repair the legs on a small Herschell-Spillman horse. Leonard tackled the assignment, enjoyed it, began attending carousel conventions, and gradually assembled an impressive list of clients.

Although it paid the bills for a number of years, repair work didn't nourish Leonard's creative soul. So he started reproducing rare carousel figures and carving original figures for collectors across the country. "Typically, people come in with a picture of a horse that they like and I'll modify it. I'll change the head and leg positions, put on a new mane and a new tail ... and it becomes a different horse designed specifically for that customer. Yet, it resembles the original," he points out.

To date, Leonard's most challenging project has been the carving of seventeen horses for a one-of-a-kind merry-go-round for *Le Carrousel de Lancelot* at Euro Disney. The giant armored carousel horses, which are 25 percent larger than most, weigh about 250 pounds each and measure six and a half feet long by seven feet high. It took over a year of round-the-clock work for Leonard and another full-time carver to finish the project on schedule. "It was crazy! We pulled ideas from all over the place. There were times that I woke up at 3:00 A.M. with the design for a horse in mind," Leonard recalls.

In 1983, Gerry Holzman of East Islip, New York, came up with the idea of creating a state carousel which would become a traveling museum of New York State's history and culture. Scheduled for completion in the fall of 1994, the Empire State Carousel will be one of the first full-sized, hand-carved carousels produced in the United States since the 1930s. With the help of three other professional carvers and close to a thousand volunteer craftspeople, the former social studies teacher has created hundreds of carvings and paintings depicting the history and folklore of New York. Included in these carvings are 30 carousel animals, all of which are indigenous to New York. Among this variety of creatures are such figures as Freddie Frogg, Clarissa Cow, Percy the Pig, Bucky the Beaver and Denny the Deermouse, who wears a cap patterned after one of Holzman's own.

"I'm not as good a carver as Daniel Müller," Holzman says. "I don't have the eyesight. I don't have the control or the artistic ability, but I do have a sense of whimsy. All of my animals have personality and character. They make people laugh."

Although his creations are whimsical, Holzman takes the art of carving seriously and identifies with the master carvers that came before him. "After a while, you begin to see the form inside the wood. It's in there and you stop when you've reached it," he explains. "Then, at a certain point, you also forget that you have tools in your hand. The tools become extensions of your hand. You feel as if you are carving with your fingers and they just happen to be very sharp. When those two things happen, you're really carving. You're a part of the tradition. It's quite a feeling."

As an ex-teacher of architectural drawing, Bill Finkenstein has always enjoyed the creative process, both in the classroom and out, but it wasn't until he was asked to use his artistic talents to restore a small horse that he found himself in an entirely new profession. That first horse soon led to the overhaul of a complete carousel from the amusement park at Lake Compounce, Connecticut. Over the past twelve years Finkenstein has built up a national reputation for his carousel restoration business, R & F Design of Bristol, Connecticut. During that time R & F has restored over a dozen complete carousels and hundreds of individual figures. "Individual figures are fun to restore," explains Finkenstein, "but when you do a whole carousel, it's like putting together a huge, wonderful jigsaw puzzle."

But there wasn't quite enough creativity in the repair of these figures, so the idea of building a carousel from scratch came to mind. The theme of endangered species was picked, and the design staff at R & F went into high gear. "This idea really allowed me to put all of my creativity—drafting, design, sculpting, and painting—into one big project," says Finkenstein. Forty-eight different animals for the carousel have been chosen, and the models have been made. Most of the full-sized figures have been carved and are ready for assembly on an old original carousel mechanism. As soon as a home is found, the carousel will be operating. Of course, if you can't afford to have an entire carousel in your backyard, R & F has built several scale models, and you'll only need a twelve-foot space to set it up.

For Leonard, Holzman, and Finkenstein, there is a direct link between them and the master carvers whose work they so admire. The age of making wooden carousels may have been dormant for many years, but if these three have their way, the creation of the hand-carved carousel may be well on the road to recovery.

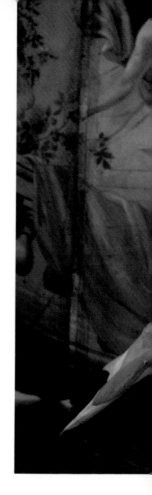

TOP: BILL FINKENSTEIN CARVES THE FULL-SIZED FIGURE O[F] THE DOLPHIN WHICH IS ABOARD THE ENDANGERED SPECIES CAROUSEL CONSTRUCTED BY R & F DESIGN.

BOTTOM: A MODEL OF THE DOLPHIN FROM THE ENDANGERED SPECIES CAROUSEL.

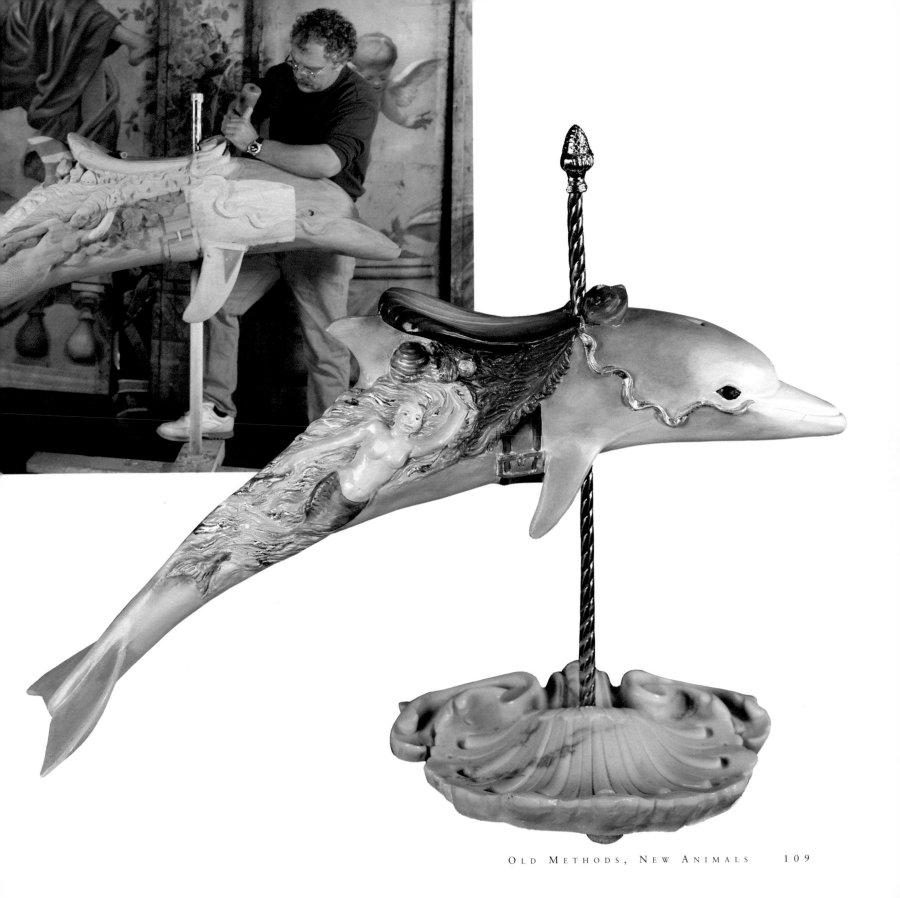

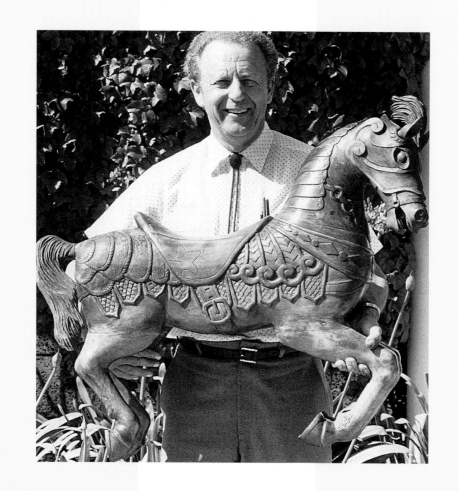

LEFT: WILLIAM (BILL) DENTZEL II HOLDS A SMALL ARMORED HORSE THAT HE CARVED IN THE MID-1980S. PHOTO: COURTESY OF MR. AND MRS. WILLIAM H. DENTZE AND FAMILY.

BELOW: A ROCKING HORSE CARVED BY BILL DENTZEL II IN THE TRADITIONAL MANNER, USING HAND TOOLS AND BLOCKS OF WOOD. PHOTO: COURTESY OF MR. AND MRS. WILLIAM H. DENTZEL AND FAMILY.

A FAMILY TRADITION CONTINUES

In the 1830s, Michael Dentzel was carving carousel figures at his shop in Kreuznach, Germany. Over 150 years later, Michael's great-great-grandson is still at it. Creating carousels has become a way of life for the Dentzel family, and although there was a period of time when the art had been lost, or perhaps just temporarily misplaced, it is back in full swing today.

Michael's son Gustav had two sons of his own. The eldest, William, was less artistic and more business-minded than his younger brother Edward, who spent many years developing his talents as a woodcarver. Eventually Edward moved west and setted in Southern California where he turned his artistic abilities toward architecture, leaving the world of carousels behind.

The next generation of Dentzels started with Edward's son William Dentzel II. Knowing only bits and pieces of the family heritage, Bill studied law and became a successful attorney before his woodcarving roots called to him. In the early 1970s he began carving as a hobby, a hobby that soon turned into a second career. His dream was to create an entirely new Dentzel carousel which would operate for the benefit of the community.

His passion for wood was passed along to his son, William Dentzel III, who has dedicated his life to the art of creating wonderful wooden carousel animals. Including the other children, David, Chris, and Barbara, the family planned an original hand-carved carousel, which is being installed in a new oceanside complex located in Santa Barbara, California. Although Bill II was not able to see the completion of his dream (he died in 1991 just as the project was getting under way), his wife, Marion, and his entire family are pitching in to make sure that his love of carousels will be appreciated by many happy riders for years to come.

MORE THAN A MERRY-GO-ROUND

❖❖❖❖❖❖❖❖❖❖❖❖❖❖❖❖❖❖❖❖❖❖❖❖❖❖❖❖

CHAPTER 10

The carousel is a simple ride. It is a compilation of gears, carved wooden figures, and a rotating platform. People buy a ticket, climb onto an animal, and for the next three minutes enjoy the sensations of whirling in a circle. Yet something odd happens when the ride is over: the rider's sensations and feelings grow and change as their memory of the carousel lasts well beyond the initial excitement of that first ride.

Because of the effect that this machine has had on us, carousels and carousel animals pop up in unexpected places. They have starred in movies and have appeared on

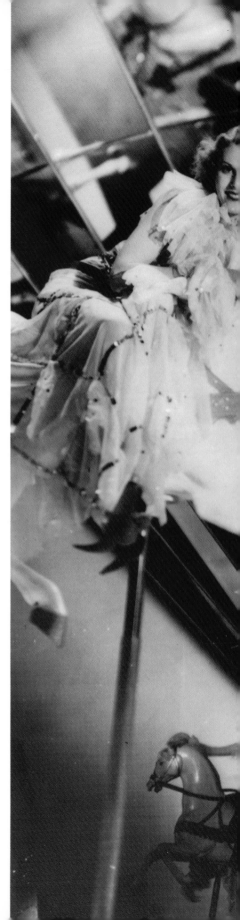

CAROUSELS OFTEN APPEARED IN MOVIES, SUCH AS THIS 1931 MUSICAL TITLED THE DANCING GIRLS. PHOTO: COURTESY OF SMITHSONIAN INSTITUTION.

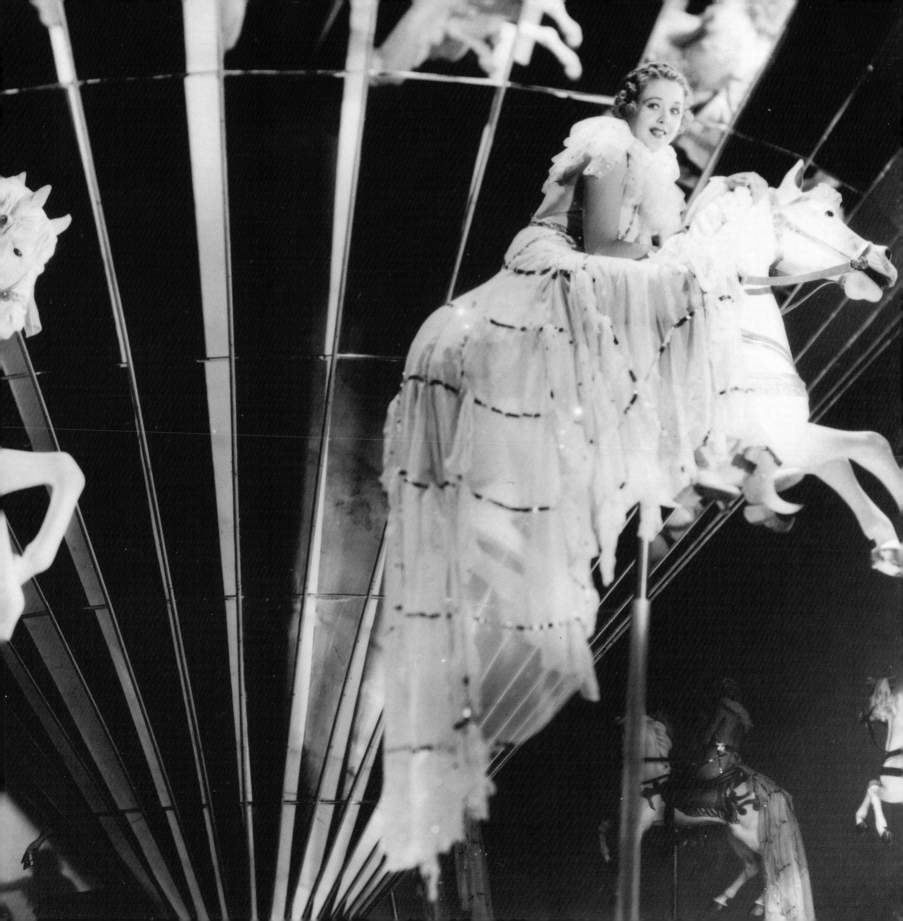

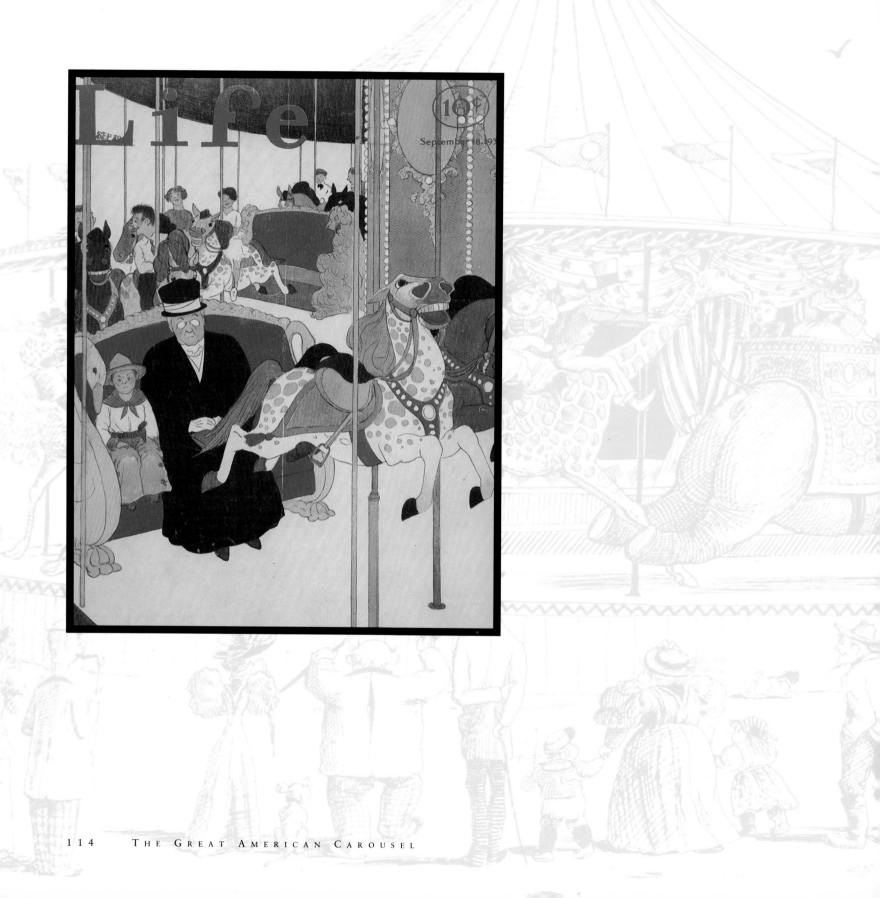

the covers of national magazines. They have been portrayed as delightful fantasy machines and as dark devices of evil. They are both romantic icons and coveted collector's items, but no matter what they have come to represent, it is certain that they have become a part of our everyday life in a way that the Dentzels, Looffs, and Herschells never expected.

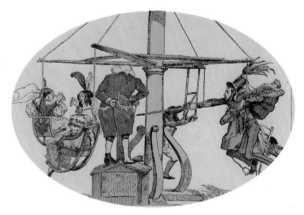

The first use of carousels outside of the realm of an amusement device was in political cartoons. The idea of going around in circles was a perfect analogy for politicians and for the social elite. If a newspaper thought that some aristocrat, senator, or even president was giving lots of speeches and saying nothing, they would inevitably place the victim on the editorial page riding a merry-go-round, complete with some derogatory notation.

As the carousel continued to grow in popularity, so did its use in other mediums. The musical scores that mention this delightful machine have been plentiful over the years. Marches and waltzes dedicated to the carousel started appearing in the nineteenth century, and the idea of the carousel in popular music has continued ever since, inspiring songwriters as diverse as Joni Mitchell, Jacques Brel, and The Coasters.

Although the image of a carousel has been evoked in dozens of songs, the crowning glory of the merry-go-round in music must certainly be Rogers and Hammerstein's tragic love story *Carousel*. The composers could not have found a better use of the carousel's image of innocence and romance than by positioning it against the harsh realities of the traveling carnival. "The Carousel Waltz," the hauntingly beautiful theme from the musical, has enjoyed even greater renown through hundreds of thousands of music boxes.

Carousels are a natural subject for artistic interpretation. Of the hundreds of artists who have sketched or painted this ride into their artwork, Norman Rockwell created what is probably the best-known image, a painting of a county fair showing the portrait of an Allan Herschell standing horse that appeared on the cover of the May 3, 1947, edition of the *Saturday Evening Post*.

BACKGROUND: THE COVER ON THE SHEET MUSIC OF THE "MERRY-GO-ROUND MARCH," PUBLISHED IN 1890. PHOTO: COURTESY OF COLLECTIONS OF THE HENRY FORD MUSEUM AND GREENFIELD VILLAGE.

INSET LEFT: THIS COVER OF LIFE MAGAZINE APPEARED ABOUT THE SAME TIME THAT THE LAST FULL-SIZED WOODEN CAROUSEL WAS BEGIN BUILT BY THE PHILADELPHIA TOBOGGAN COMPANY. PHOTO: COURTESY OF NEW YORK PUBLIC LIBRARY.

UPPER RIGHT: A SATIRICAL COMMENTARY ON THE FRENCH ARISTOCRACY SHOWS THE TWO DAUGHTERS OF KING LOUIS-PHILIPPE BEING PURSUED BY THE DUKE OF ORLEANS IN AN ATTEMPT TO MARRY ONE OF THEM. PHOTO: COURTESY OF NEW YORK PUBLIC LIBRARY.

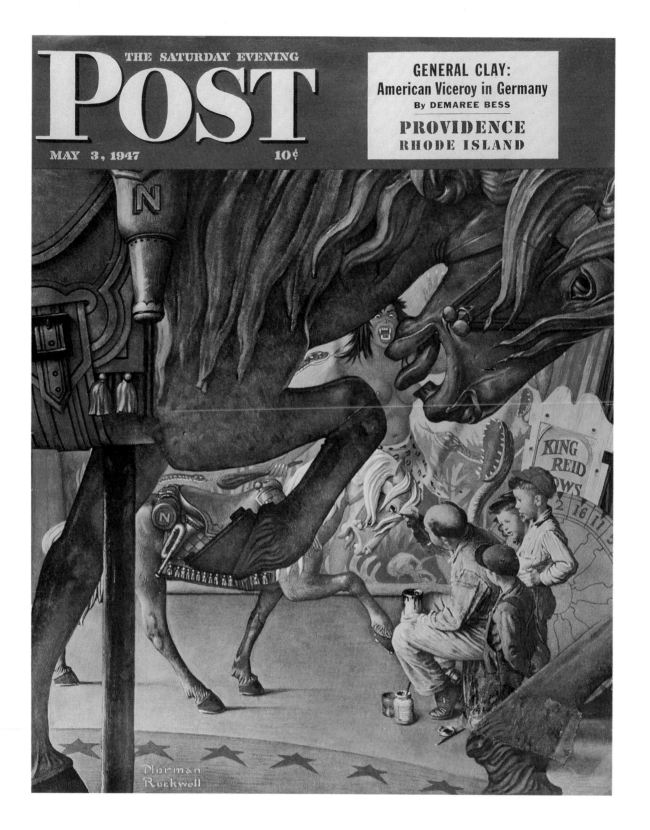

Even Norman Rockwell used carousels in a number of his paintings, including this 1941 Saturday Evening Post illustration showing an early carousel restorer working at a carnival. The horse used as a model for this painting resided on Rockwell's front porch for many years. Collection of Roland and Jo Summit.

Carousels have been featured in dozens of movies and there are several instances where they have achieved star status. Their first major role was in Alfred Hitchcock's *Strangers on a Train*, where the final scene finds the good guy battling the bad guy on an out-of-control Allan Herschell traveling machine. Carousels were costars in *The Sting* (the Philadelphia Toboggan Company's carousel at the Santa Monica Pier), *Mary Poppins* (Disney animated horses), Clint Eastwood's *Sudden Impact* (Charles Looff's machine at the Boardwalk in Santa Cruz, California), and, of course, the screen adaptation of Ray Bradbury's *Something Wicked This Way Comes* (C. W. Parker).

Rarely has a part of our artistic heritage become so ingrained in public life. From children's books to advertising to the amusement park, the carousel is with us in some way almost every day.

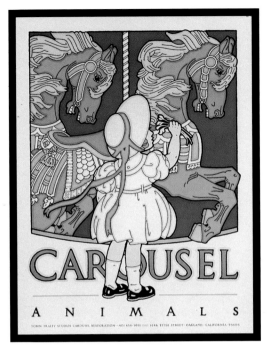

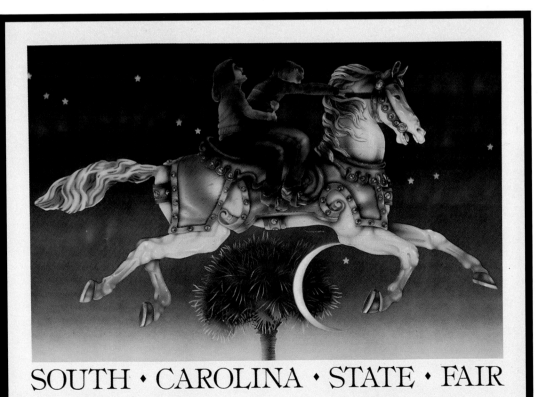

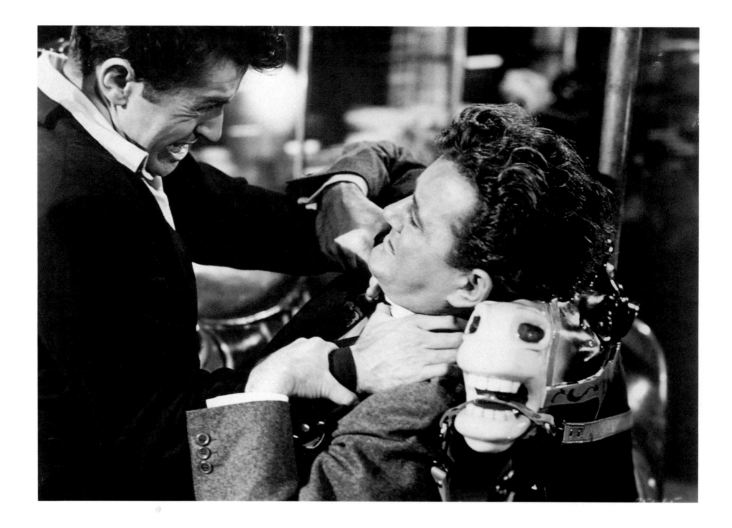

THE FINAL SCENE FROM ALFRED HITCHCOCK'S 1951 CLASSIC,
STRANGERS ON A TRAIN, TAKES PLACE ON A WHIRLING
CAROUSEL AS FARLEY GRANGER AND ROBERT WALKER BATTLE
EACH OTHER.

ON CAROUSEL DECORATION

On carousels, most of the references to subjects of the day were left up to the artists who painted the scenery panels and rounding boards. On their canvases they would paint idyllic scenes of strolling Victorian ladies or vast pastoral landscapes. Sometimes the images would become a bit livelier with the portrayal of hunting scenes or a view of the Wild West. The only exceptions were communications to the riders, about the cost of a ticket or the name of the maker who had created the wonderful machine they were riding.

On rare occasions, the carvers themselves looked to what was currently popular for inspiration. Most common were expressions of pride in a newfound country, such as the creation of an American flag on an animal's side. Abraham Lincoln was honored several times when his portrait was added to trappings of a horse. But the most renowned is a Dentzel tiger sporting the likeness of a uniformed Teddy Roosevelt charging up San Juan Hill.

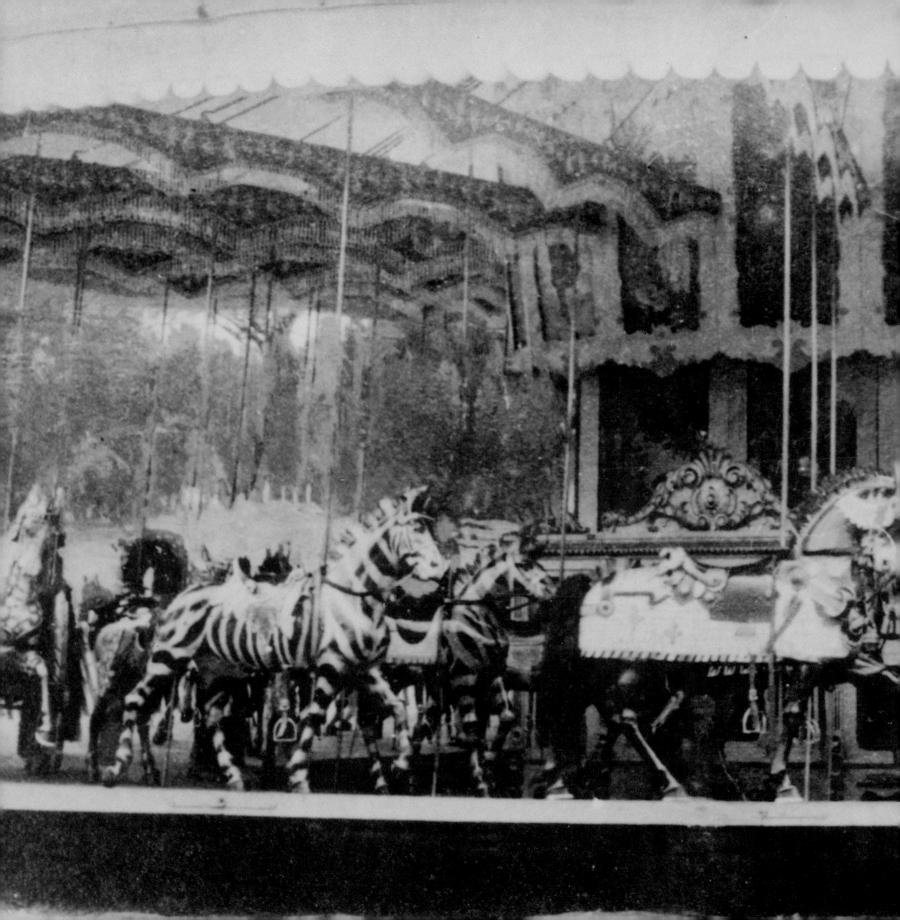

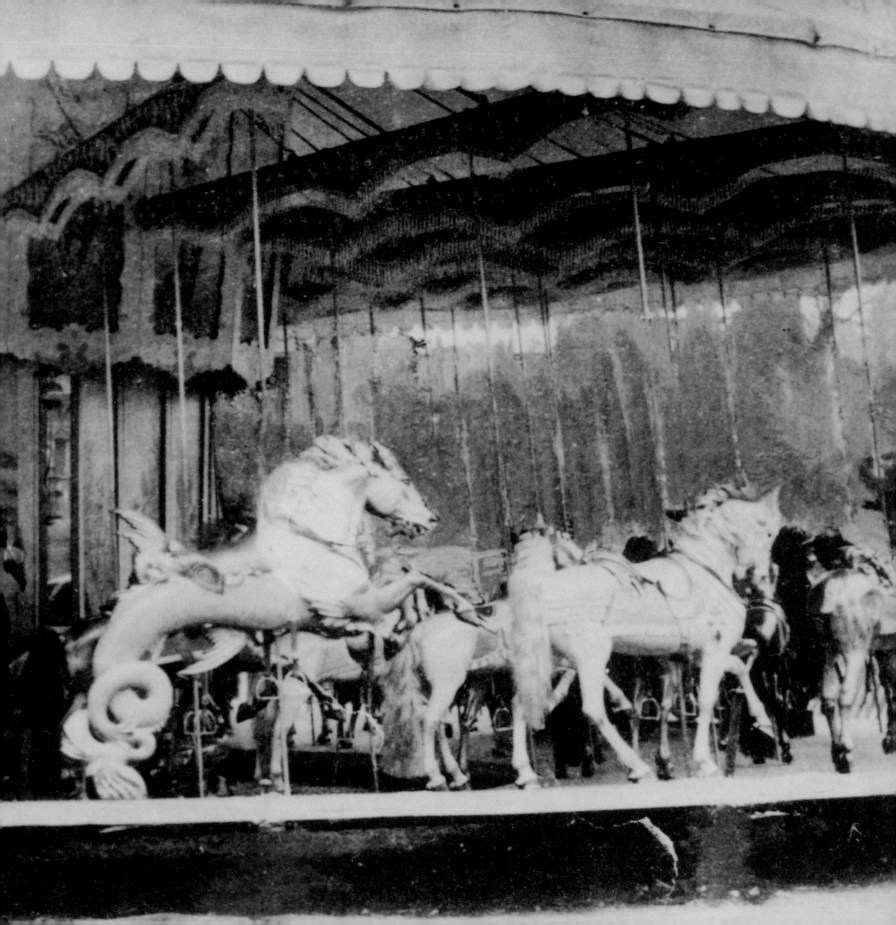

Afterword

There were days growing up in my grandfather's park when the August sky was so blue and the morning air so clean that it seemed as if I could touch everything I saw without taking a step. I knew that I owned those days, and I went out to greet them with the exuberance that only an eight-year-old can have. It would be hours before the gates opened to the public; until then the place was mine. I would sprint across the vast lawn that separated this horseshoe of a park from Bitter Lake. As I ran, the grass that still held drops from the night's layer of dew was drenching the canvas sides of my Keds Hi-Tops. ❧ I made a bee-line to Grandpa's office, where, more likely than not, I would find him putting the finishing touches on some scrambled eggs and bacon. Outside, the hum of activity had already begun. The clean-up crews were tending to the debris from the night before, and soon the ride operators would be putting the Tilt-A-Whirl, the Rock-O-Plane, and the Whip through their daily trial runs. When breakfast was over, Grandpa grabbed his hat and we were out the door. ❧ Which direction I went depended on who or what I saw first. Sometimes I would see my father heading toward the merry-go-round, so off I went. Everything needed to be checked and rechecked. The gears might need greasing, or perhaps there was a loose bolt waiting to be tightened. At some point it was time for the engine to be tested. As soon as the switch was thrown, the hum of the big electric motor mingled with the flapping of the

PRECEDING PAGES: WHEN THE MÜLLER BROTHERS SET UP THEIR OWN SHOP, THEY NEEDED AN ANNOUNCEMENT TO SEND TO POTENTIAL CUSTOMERS. PUTTING TOGETHER ONE OF THEIR FIRST CAROUSELS IN THE BACK OF THEIR FACTORY, THEY PHOTOGRAPHED IT, LATER PAINTING IN A BACKGROUND OF TREES AND SKY TO MAKE THE SETTING MORE APPEALING. PHOTO: COURTESY OF SMITHSONIAN INSTITUTION.

belts. The mechanical, almost sweet smell of heavy oil filled the air as I stood transfixed in the center of the

great machine, surrounded by an array of unfathomable gears, cranks, and rods. ❧ When the time came

to open the gates, the crowds had already gathered and were waiting to spill through the turnstiles. The daytime

revelers were mostly families. I would lose myself in the throngs, becoming one of an endless number of kids,

except for the secret. After years of study and observation, I was certain that I was the only person in the park

who knew the number on the absolutely fastest of the bumper cars. I would wait until there were enough peo-

ple to have a really spirited ride, then, making sure that I was first in line, I would hop into old #12 and prepare

to make mincemeat out of those unknowing riders who made the uninformed assumption that all bumper cars

are the same. ❧ As dinnertime rolled around, families began to pack up, and the crowd of people began to

thin, making way for the slightly older and a bit more raucous evening patrons. I made my way back home,

sometimes stopping by the lake to throw a few bits of bread to the mallards that would flock to your feet when

tempted by a free meal. ❧ The apartment where my family lived that year was behind the games building. At

night, the popping of the balloons as darts found their marks mixed with the clatter of metal milk bottles crash-

ing as some new pitching ace dazzled his date with a fastball. The clanking sound of the roller coaster echoed

throughout the park as the row of little red cars drew ever closer to the precipice. There was always a moment

when the clanking stopped, just before the riders were catapulted over the edge and began their shrieks of glee-

ful fear at that uneasy sense of weightlessness. But more than anything the sounds of the crowds, that unending

murmur that rose and fell like waves against the sand, washed over me in the still air of that back room. ❧

On occasion, my family would travel to other amusement parks. And even though I spent my summer days

racing around on familiar bumper cars or riding in endless circles on our carousel, I would still go directly to the *ticket booths at these parks so that I could buy a whole batch of ride coupons. The day was not complete until I had the experience of waiting patiently in line for the chance to board their carousel filled with wooden creatures different from the ones I knew so well. As I waited I would try to pick out the best one. Would I find the fastest or the fiercest one? Which one would I rush to as soon as the gates opened? What was my second choice if someone in front of me had picked the same animal? All of these thoughts went through my mind. Sometimes it seemed to take an eternity for everyone to finally dismount and leave after the previous ride was over, but at last the gates opened and I rushed onto the carousel, scrambling atop the horse I had picked. ❧*

Over the melody of a Strauss waltz pouring forth from the Wurlitzer band organ, three clear clangs on the large brass bell rang out their signal to hold on. The man in the center released the brake while slowly engaging the clutch. A slight shudder was felt throughout the great carousel as the flowered prancers, fiery steeds, and jungle beasts began their journey. By the third time around, the world outside the carousel became a blur, and the imaginations of all aboard were transported to times and places seen only in our dreams.

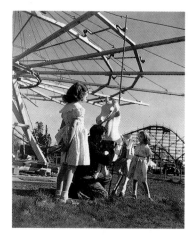

THE AUTHOR'S FATHER, MAURICE FRALEY, PREPARING A
DENTZEL HORSE FOR OPENING DAY IN 1955.

Bibliography

Braithwaite, Patrick. *Savage of King's Lynn*. Cambridge, England: Stephens Publisher, 1975.

Dinger, Charlotte. *Art of the Carousel*. Green Village, NJ: Carousel Art, 1983.
[*N.B.* Carousel Art, P.O. Box 150, Green Village, NJ, 07935.]

Fraley, Nina. *The American Carousel*. Benecia, CA: Redbug Publishing, 1979.

Fraley, Tobin. *The Carousel Animal*. San Francisco, CA: Chronicle Books, 1983.

Fried, Frederick. *A Pictorial History of the Carousel*. Vestal, NY: Vestal Press, Ltd., 1964.
[*N.B.* Vestal Press, Ltd., P.O. Box 97, 320 North Jenson Road, Vestal, NY, 13850.]

Hinds, Anne Dion. *Grab the Brass Ring*. New York: Crown Publishers, 1990.

Mangels, William F. *Outdoor Amusement Industry*. New York: Vantage Press, 1952

McCullough, Edo. *Good Old Coney Island*. New York: Charles Scribner's Sons, 1957.

Shank, Peggy. *Painted Ponies*. Millwood, NY: Zon Publishing, 1986.

Summit, Roland. *Carousels of Coney Island*. Rolling Hills, CA: Roland Summit, 1970.

Swenson, Marge. *Carrousel Art Magazine* (Garden Grove, CA), 1978–1988.
[*N.B.* Carousel Art, P.O. Box 992, Garden Grove, CA, 92642.]

Weedon, Geoff, and Richard Ward. *Fairground Art*. New York, NY: Abbeville Press, 1981.

Williams, Barbara. "John Zalar, Master Carver," *Merry-Go-Roundup Quarterly*, Spring 1979.

Carousel News & Trader Magazine (Mansfield, OH), 1985–1994.
[*N.B. Carousel News & Trader Magazine*, 87 Park Avenue West, #206, Mansfield, OH, 44902.
Phone (419) 529-4999.]

California

Anaheim - Disneyland, Dentzel/Looff/Carmel mix, c. 1920.

Berkeley - Tilden Park, Herschell-Spillman Company, c. 1911.

Buena Park - Knott's Berry Farm, Dentzel Company, c. 1902.

City of Industry - Puente Hills Mall, Philadelphia Toboggan Company #15, c. 1907.

Long Beach - Shoreline Village, Charles Looff, c. 1906.

Los Angeles - Griffith Park, Spillman Engineering Corp., with some Looff and Carmel horses, c. 1926.

San Diego - Balboa Park, Herschell-Spillman Company, c. 1910.

San Diego - Seaport Village, Charles Looff, c. 1890.

San Francisco - Golden Gate Park, Herschell-Spillman Company, c. 1912.

San Francisco - San Francisco Zoo, Dentzel Company with some Illions figures, c. 1921.

Santa Clara - Great America, Philadelphia Toboggan Company #45, c. 1918.

Santa Cruz - Santa Cruz Beach Boardwalk, Charles Looff, c. 1911.

Santa Monica - Santa Monica Pier, Philadelphia Toboggan Company #62, c. 1922.

Valencia - Six Flags Magic Mountain, Philadelphia Toboggan Company #21, c. 1912.

Colorado

Burlington - Kit Carson County Fairgrounds, Philadelphia Toboggan Company #62, c. 1905.

Denver - Elitch Gardens, Philadelphia Toboggan Company #51, c. 1925.

Denver - Lakeside Park, C. W. Parker Amusement Company, c. 1908.

Connecticut

Bristol - Lake Compounce Festival Park, Carmel/Looff/Stein & Goldstein mix, c. 1893–1910.

Hartford - Bushnell Park, Stein & Goldstein, c. 1914.

New Haven - Lighthouse Point Park, Carmel/Looff mix, c. 1911.

District of Columbia

Washington - The Mall at the Smithsonian Institution, Allan Herschell Company, c. 1947.

Washington - Washington Cathedral, U.S. Merry-Go-Round Company, c. 1913.

Florida

Kissammee - Old Town, Looff/Stein & Goldstein/Carmel mix, c. 1909.

Lake Buena Vista - Walt Disney World, Philadelphia Toboggan Company #46, c. 1917.

Tampa - Tampa Bay Center, Spillman Engineering Corp., c. 1922.

Georgia

Atlanta - Six Flags Over Georgia, Philadelphia Toboggan Company #17, c. 1908.

Rossville - Lake Winnepesaukah Park, Philadelphia Toboggan Company #39, c. 1916.

Idaho

Rexburg - Porter Park, Spillman Engineering Corp., c. 1926.

Illinois

Gurnee - Six Flags Great America, Dentzel Company, c. 1910.

Melrose Park - Kiddieland, Philadelphia Toboggan Company #72, c. 1925.

Indiana

Indianapolis - The Children's Museum, Dentzel Company, c. 1900.

Indianapolis - Indianapolis Zoo, C. W. Parker Amusement Company, c. 1910.

Logansport - Riverside Park, Dentzel Company, c. 1902.

Kansas

Abilene - Heritage Center, C. W. Parker Amusement Company, c. 1901.

Leavenworth - Leavenworth Historical Museum, C. W. Parker Amusement Company, c. 1913.

Topeka - Gage Park, Herschell-Spillman Company, c. 1908.

Wichita - Cowtown Park, Armitage-Herschell Company, c. 1894.

Louisiana

New Orleans - New Orleans City Park, Looff/Carmel mix, c. 1906.

Maine

Newfield - Willowbrook at Newfield, Armitage-Herschell Company, c. 1894.

Old Orchard Beach - Palace Playland, Philadelphia Toboggan Company #19, c. 1908.

Maryland

Baltimore - Harbor Place at Inner Harbor, Herschell-Spillman Company, c. 1912.

Glen Echo - Glen Echo Park, Dentzel Company, c. 1921.

Ocean City - Windsor Resort, Herschell-Spillman Company, c. 1908.

Upper Marlboro - Watkins Regional Park, Dentzel Company, c. 1895–1920.

Wheaton - Wheaton Regional Park, Herschell-Spillman Company, c. 1910.

Massachusetts

Agawam - Riverside Park, M. C. Illions & Sons, c. 1911.

Fall River - Heritage State Park, Philadelphia Toboggan Company #54, c. 1920.

Holyoke - Mountain Park, Philadelphia Toboggan Company #80, c. 1927.

Hull - Carousel Under the Clock, Philadelphia Toboggan Company #85, 1928.

Oak Bluffs - Flying Horses of Martha's Vineyard, C. W. Dare Company, c. 1876.

Sandwich - Heritage Plantation, Charles Looff, c. 1902.

Michigan

Dearborn - Henry Ford Museum and Greenfield Village, Herschell-Spillman Company, c. 1912.

Flint - Historic Crossroads Village, C. W. Parker Amusement Company, c. 1912.

Grand Rapids - Grand Rapids Public Museum, Spillman Engineering Corp., c. 1928.

Minnesota

Saint Paul - Town Square Park, Philadelphia Toboggan Company #33, c. 1914.

Shakopee - Valleyfair Family Amusement Park, Philadelphia Toboggan Company #76, c. 1926.

Mississippi

Meridian - Highland Park, Dentzel Company, c. 1909.

Missouri

Chesterfield - Faust County Park, Armitage-Herschell Company, c. 1898.

Chesterfield - Faust County Park, Dentzel Company, c. 1920.

Eureka - Six Flags Over Mid-America, Philadelphia Toboggan Company #35, c. 1915.

Independence - Independence Center Mall, Spillman Engineering Corp., c. 1920.

New Hampshire

Salem - Canobie Lake Park, Looff/Stein & Goldstein/Dentzel mix, c. 1906.

New Jersey

Ocean City - Wonderland Pier, Philadelphia Toboggan Company #75, c. 1926.

Seaside Heights - Casino Pier, Illions/Dentzel/Looff mix, c. 1909.

New York

Baldwin - Nunley's Amusement Park, Stein & Goldstein, c. 1910.

Binghamton - Recreation Park, Allan Herschell Company, c. 1925.

Binghamton - Ross Park Zoo, Allan Herschell Company, c. 1920.

Brooklyn - Coney Island, Charles Carmel, c. 1912.

Brooklyn - Prospect Park, Charles Carmel, c. 1914.

Endicott - George W. Johnson Park, Allan Herschell Company, c. 1934.

Johnson City - C. Fred Johnson Recreational Park, Allan Herschell Company, c. 1923.

New York/Manhattan - Central Park, Stein & Goldstein, c. 1908.

New York/Queens - Flushing Meadows/Corona Park, M. C. Illions & Sons, c. 1905.

New York/Queens - Forest Park, D. C. Müller and Bro., c. 1910.

North Tonawanda - Herschell Carrousel Factory Museum, Allan Herschell Company, c. 1916.

Rochester - Ontario Beach Park, Dentzel Company, c. 1905.

Rochester - Sea Breeze Park, Philadelphia Toboggan Company #36, c. 1915.

Rye - Rye Playland Park, Charles Carmel, c. 1911.

Rye - Rye Playland Park, Prior & Church Racing Derby, c. 1926.

Syracuse - Carousel Center Mall, Philadelphia Toboggan Company #18, c. 1909.

North Carolina

Burlington - Burlington City Park, Dentzel Company, c. 1917.

Charlotte - Carowinds Amusement Park, Philadelphia Toboggan Company #67, c. 1923.

Raleigh - Chavis Park, Allan Herschell Company, c. 1925.

Raleigh - Pullen Park, Dentzel Company, c. 1910.

North Dakota

Wahpeton - Chahinkapa Zoo, Spillman Engineering Corp., c. 1926.

Ohio

Aurora - Geauga Lake, M. C. Illions & Sons, c. 1918.

Kings Mills - Kings Island Amusement Park, Philadelphia Toboggan Company #79, c. 1926.

Powell - Wyandot Lake Amusement Park, M. C. Illions & Sons, c. 1914.

Put-In-Bay - City Center Park, Allan Herschell Company, c. 1917.

Sandusky - Cedar Point Amusement Park (four carousels), Dentzel Company, c. 1921; Prior & Church Racing Derby, c. 1922; D. C. Müller and Bro., c. 1912; and Dentzel Company, c. 1924.

Oregon

Portland - Jantzen Beach Center, C. W. Parker Amusement Company, c. 1917.·

Portland - Oaks Amusement Park, Herschell-Spillman Company, c. 1924.

Pennsylvania

Albion - Albion Boro Park, U.S. Merry-Go-Round Company, c. 1890.

Elysburg - Knoebels Grove Amusement Resort (two carousels), Charles Carmel, c. 1912; and Stein & Goldstein, c. 1910.

Hershey - Hershey Park, Philadelphia Toboggan Company #47, c. 1919.

Ligonier - Idlewild Park, Philadelphia Toboggan Company #83, c. 1924.

Pen Argyl - Weona Park, Dentzel Company, c. 1917.

West Mifflin - Kennywood Park, Dentzel Company, c. 1926.

Rhode Island

East Providence - Carousel Park (formerly Crescent Park) Charles Looff, c. 1904.

Watch Hill - Watch Hill Park, C. W. Dare Company, c. 1885.

Tennessee

Memphis - Libertyland, Dentzel Company, c. 1921.

Pigeon Forge - Dollywood, Dentzel Company, c. 1902.

Texas

Arlington - Six Flags Over Texas, Dentzel Company, c. 1926.

Dallas - Fair Park/County Fairgrounds, Dentzel Company, c. 1914.

Houston - Astroworld, Dentzel Company/D. C. Müller and Bro. mix, c. 1907.

Utah

Farmington - Lagoon Park, Herschell-Spillman Company, c. 1906.

Virginia

Doswell - Kings Dominion Amusement Park, Philadelphia Toboggan Company #44, c. 1917.

Hampton - Hampton Waterfront Park, Philadelphia Toboggan Company #50, c. 1920.

Williamsburg - Busch Gardens, Allan Herschell Company, c. 1919.

Washington

Puyallup - Western Washington Fair, Philadelphia Toboggan Company #43, c. 1917.

Spokane - Riverfront Park, Charles Looff, c. 1909.

American Carousel Museum, 633 Beach Street, San Francisco, CA 94109; (415) 928-0550.

Carousel World/Peddler's Village, Route 202 at Route 263, Lahaska, PA 18931; (215) 794-8960.

Circus World Museum, 426 Water Street, Baraboo, WI 53913; (608) 356-8341.

Dickinson County Historical Society, 412 South Campbell, Abilene, KS 67410; (913) 263-2681.

Empire State Carousel, Brookwood Hall, 86 Cedar Avenue, East Islip, NY 11751; (516) 277-6168.

Heritage Plantation, Grove Street, Sandwich, MA 02563; (508) 888-3300.

Herschell Carrousel Factory Museum, 180 Thompson Street, N. Tonawanda, NY 14120; (716) 693-1885.

Indianapolis Children's Museum, 30th at Meridian, Indianapolis, IN 46208; (317) 924-5431.

Merry-Go-Round Museum, West Washington at Jackson Street, Sandusky, OH 44870; (419) 626-6111.

New England Carousel Museum, 95 Riverside Avenue, Bristol, CT 06010; (203) 585-5411.

Shelburne Museum, Route 7, Shelburne, VT 05482; (802) 985-3346.

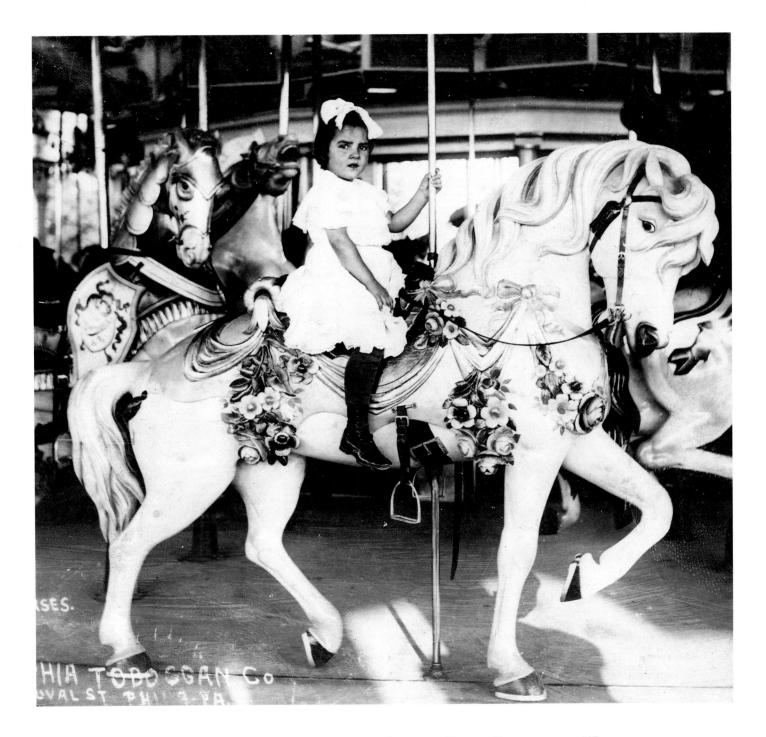

A GRAND FLOWERED OUSIDE-ROW STANDER FROM PHILADELPHIA TOBOGGAN COMPANY CAROUSEL #17
AT RIVERVIEW PARK IN CHICAGO, C. 1912. PHOTOGRAPH: COURTESY OF STAPLES & CHARLES.

Index

Page numbers in italic indicate
photographs

Albright, Chester, *52*

Allan Herschell Company, 56, *62*, 87

American Merry-Go-Round &
  Novelty Company, The, 31

Armitage, James, 31, 36

Armitage-Herschell Company, 36, 44

Artistic Caroussel Manufacturing
  Company, 34, 50, 70

Auchy, Henry, *41*, 52, 81

Borrelli, M. D., 50

Bungarz Steam Wagon & Carrousele
  Works, The, 31

C. W. Parker Amusement Company,
  36, 52, 54, 70

Carmel, Charles, 50, *51*, 70, 72

Carousel craftsmen
  background of, 12
  techniques, 61–67

Carousel industry
  apprenticeships, 78

economic changes, 44, 56, 87–88

Carousel
  decoration, 119
  etymology & origins, 18, 20, 34
  manufacturers, 31–36
  mechanics of, 25
  in modern culture, 112–18
  rediscovery of, 88–90
  restoration, 96–103
  steam powered, 21

Carretta, Frank, *57*, 70, 87

Cedar Point Amusement Park, 87

Cernigliaro, Salvatore, 64, 70–71, 74,
  82, 87

Charles W. Dare Company, 32

Coney Island, 32, *41*, 50

Contemporary carvers, 104–11

D. C. Müller and Bro., 70, 56, 82–83
  carousel, *121*
  creation of, 52

Dare, Charles, 31–34, 36

Dentzel Company, 28, 43, 52, 83, 99

Dentzel II, William, *110*, 111

Dentzel, Gustav, 9, *31*, 36, 78,
  81–82, 111
  carousel business (U.S.), 31, 44

Dentzel, Michael, 31

Dentzel, William, 56, 82

Dolle, Fred, 50

Drisco, Eugene, 70

E. Joy Morris Carousel Company,
  52, 70

Finkenstein, Bill, 104, 108, 109

Fraley, Tobin, *15*

Fried, Frederick, 88

Goldstein, Harry, 34, 50, 70

Grafly, Charles, 81

Herschell, Allan, 31, 36, 99

Herschell-Spillman Company, 10, *42*,
  46–47, 52, 56, 63, 86
  variety of figures, 44–47

Herschell-Spillman traveling carousel,
  56–57

Holzman, Gerry, 104, *106*, 107–8

Illions, Marcus Charles, 13, *20*, *48*,
  62, *73*, 86, 87

restoration at Coney Island, 49

Kilcullen, Patrick, 81–82

Kopp, C. F., *60*

Kraus, Ernst, 82

Leonard, Joe, 104, *106*, 107

Leopold, Charles, 69, 70, 82

Looff, Charles, *37*, *43*, 50, 56, 78, 89

   carousel business (U.S.), 31–34

Looff carousel, *45*, *88*

Luna Park, *38*

M. C. Illions and Sons, 70, 73

Mangels Carousel Works, 50

Mangels, William, 49, 50

Morris, E. Joy, 81

Morton, Will, 99, 102–3

Müller, Alfred, 28, 52, 78, 79

Müller, Daniel, 13, *30*, 63, 65,
   76–81, 83, 87

   and Dentzel Company, 82

   life and work, 76–83

   and Philadelphia Toboggan
     Company, 81–82

   work for Henry Auchy, 52

Müller, Johann (or John), *28*, 76–78

Murphy, Thomas, 50

National Carousel Association,
   16, 90

New York Carousel Manufacturing
   Company, 32

Norman & Evans, 31

Nottingham Goose Fair, *26–27*

Parker Carnival Supply Company, 36

Parker, Charles W., 34, 36, *53–55*, 99

Philadelphia Toboggan Company, 45,
   56, *57*, *87–88*,

   beginnings, 52, 81–83

   carousels, *6–7*, *40*, *92*, *93*

Playland, 16

Ragan, Rosa, 97, 99, *100*, 101

Savage, Fredrick, 21–22

   carousel, *37*

Sea Breeze Park, *40*, 90

Spillman Engineering Corporation,
   56, *60*

Steam and Horsepower Caroussell
   Builder, 34

Stein and Goldstein, 50, 51

Stein, Soloman, 34, 50, *51*, 70

Surf Avenue, *41*

Tilden Park carousel, *42*

U.S. Caroussell and Amusement
   Company, 82

Young's Pier, 32

Zalar, John, *43*, 70, 73–75

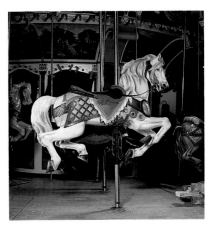

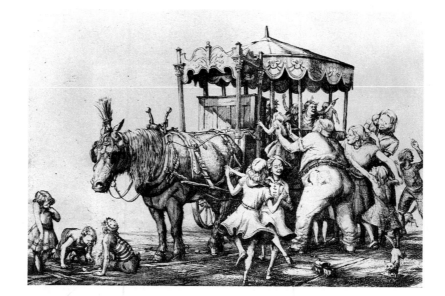

Franklin Roosevelt's **WPA** art projects included recording a variety of scenes from around the country. This artist chose as subject matter a small portable carousel that traveled from street to street entertaining the neighborhood children before moving onto the next block. Collection of the Museum of the City of New York.